"Whether you are studying the birth of our cities in the 1870s or today, there is no place where the story of the American immigrant is more fascinating than Fargo-Moorhead. These young Fargoans put a human face to topics like immigration and refugee resettlement that are often talked about right now but too seldom really explored. But a century from now, these essays will be important primary sources for future Americans to study the Lhotshampa diaspora from Nepal to North Dakota, childhood in refugee camps, life as a high school kid in 2017, or what it was like for great-grandma when she came to America from Sudan."

—**Markus Krueger, programming director,**
Historical and Cultural Society of Clay County

"We as a country are engaged in a great struggle for our identity as a welcoming place, especially since the last election. During this time, the Green Card Voices have become the voices of our conscience. These voices give first-person accounts of the memorable journeys, strong wills against all odds, and compelling life stories of young new Americans. Without these voices, we lose the raison d'être for our immigrant society that provides safety and support so people can reach higher."

—**Malini Srivastava, assistant professor of architecture,**
North Dakota State University; principal at Design and Energy Laboratory;
project lead, efargo

"What a fantastic, straightforward, and honest book. *Green Card Youth Voices* is game-changing."

—**Dr. Yuri R. Nakasato, Chair of Rheumatology Department,**
Sanford Health

"Impeccable narratives that provide a priceless opportunity to be part of the immigrants' and refugees' lifeworld. Their stories will broaden your understanding as well as shape your perspective. What an insightful read!"

—**Jonix Knight Owino, sociologist**

"The stories in *Green Card Youth Voices* are authentic and real-life experiences of young immigrants. They reflect the journeys of immigrants from diverse backgrounds with the desire to learn, share, connect, and adjust to new life in United States. Everything in the world is interconnected, interdependent, and interactive. Their voices are 'ur' voices which resonate that there is 'unity in diversity.'"

—**Yoke Sim Gunaratne, executive director, Cultural Diversity Resources**

"There's something magical that happens when reading through this book. The power of *Green Card Youth Voices* is its ability to transport you to these other places and to re-experience our own world from a new perspective. Reading about the lives of these young people reminds us of our own humanity, of the struggles they endure for the things we sometimes take for granted. It's a rare opportunity to get the perspective of being an immigrant to the US and, more importantly, on what it means to be an American and a citizen of the world. Their bravery and insight is a message that everyone should experience."

—**Raul Gomez, publisher, High Plains Reader**

"Powerful. An incredible opportunity to share our humanity. The struggles and successes of immigrants and refugees and those who were here before are America's powerful story. *Green Card Youth Voices* adds an incredible opportunity for our newest neighbors to share their fears, their hopes, their lives. In this book we share our humanity"

—**John Rodenbiker, board member, Fargo Public Schools Board of Education**

"*Green Card Youth Voices* captures and conveys powerful stories of individual journeys of hope and struggle for a better life. These are tearful recollections of trauma, insightful observations of adapting to new environments, and overall, important reflections of our common humanity."

—**Andrew Maus, director/CEO, Plains Art Museum**

"Everyone has a story. *Green Card Youth Voices* captures the powerful stories of immigrant students attending Fargo South High School. The journeys that these young men and women have experienced are a must-read. A whole new world is exposed and shared because of these ambassadors."

—**Dr. Todd Bertsch, principal, Fargo South High School**

"*Green Card Youth Voices: Immigration Stories from a Fargo High School* gives us heartfelt glimpses into the world that has come to us. It's personal, provocative, and empowering. Read it and then share it."

—**John Strand, city commissioner, City of Fargo**

"A must-read for anyone who wants to go beyond the headlines and really see people for who they are. Youth voices *always* deserve to be heard. Without a doubt this collection of stories will leave you wanting to hear more."

—**Jessica Thomasson, CEO, Lutheran Social Services of ND, Lutheran Social Services Housing**

"Immigrant Development Center supports the work of Green Card Voices and we see it as so valuable in representing the voices in our community. Thank you for doing this here in Fargo-Moorhead."

—**Fowzia Adde, executive director, Immigrant Development Center**

"If we are to address the world's greatest need before we can solve other problems, then we must address the need for building empathy between people. We must learn to see, hear, appreciate, and respect others, since we are each different. *Green Card Youth Voices* helps us hear the voices of young people who have come from around this world and make up the diverse mosaic that is the USA. These are the voices of innocence and experience, fear and hope, playfulness and purpose. If we listen, we will learn many important lessons from these young people, most of all why we should welcome them. They will bring us more than they ever demand, if we but listen and respond. I can imagine many classrooms that could use this collection of stories from real people to open eyes and minds, making us all better citizens of the USA and the world."

—**Dr. Dawn Duncan, professor of English, Film & Global Studies, Concordia College-Moorhead, MN; Narrative 4 international ambassador**

"*Green Card Youth Voices: Immigration Stories from a Fargo High School* shares stories and experiences every American needs to read."

—**Dr. Kevin Brooks, community organizer and professor of English, North Dakota State University**

"At a time when race relations have become inflamed, diversity has been challenged, and the future of immigration and immigrants in the US has been threatened, along comes *Green Card Youth Voices: Immigration Stories from a Fargo High School*. The authentic, candid accounts of these resilient young men and women, and the adversities they encountered, will change the way you perceive immigrants and the process of immigration."

—**Peggy Pulst, EL instructor, Judge Ronald N. Davies High School, Fargo, ND**

"This book is wonderful, timely and important. It speaks to stories of children survivors of unimaginable and difficult journeys to their new home, the United States. As new North Dakotans, these children are a part of the state and national fabric, and their individual histories are beautiful pieces of the puzzle that is America."

—**Anna Astvatsaturian Turcotte, author, human rights activist, politician**

Green Card Youth Voices

Immigration Stories from a Fargo High School

ISBN 13: 978-0-9974960-2-4
eISBN 13: 978-0-9974960-4-8
LCCN: 2016961598

Printed in the United States of America
Second Printing: 2017
20 19 18 17   5 4 3 2

Cover design by Elena Dodevska
Interior design by José Guzmán
Photography, videography by Media Active: Youth Produced Media

Wise Ink Creative Publishing
837 Glenwood Ave.
Minneapolis, MN 55405
www.wiseinkpub.com

To the young authors of this book, their continued safety,
the communities that welcome and support them, and the
hope that they will thrive in their new home.

Table of Contents

Foreword

"I believe that one can never leave home. I believe that one carries the shadows, the dreams, the fears and the dragons of home under one's skin, at the extreme corners of one's eyes and possibly in the gristle of the earlobe."
~ Maya Angelou

After floating in the clouds for thousands of miles, I stepped off the plane and silently prayed, "The land of the free and the home of the brave: here I come." Leaving home for another continent was a rite of passage I never dreamed of undertaking. Not when I was a little girl with braided hair and layered clothes, playing jump rope with my girlfriends in Ethiopia. Not ever.

My vivid memory of growing up in Ethiopia never seems to diminish in intensity with time. A place I proudly called home. A place where I spent the most formative years of my life. A place and a time where the phrase "being in a hurry" was not known. These memories are the anchor points of my life, the framework of my being, and the fabric of who I am. Masterfully traversing between two distinct languages and bridging the chasm between two rich cultures becomes a way of life, an immigrant's experience.

I understand the journeys traversed in this book. As ancient as the migration of people from one place to another, the toll it takes on the immigrant's soul, and the permanent hole it leaves in one's heart are profound. To step into the unknown, after separating from everything familiar, requires a great balancing act. Leaving behind loved ones who helped shape my life was more than scary. My mother's prayers and blessings have served as the wind beneath my wings.

But migration also brings with it a profound opportunity to be made anew. A fresh start. Especially in a place where such possibility is ingrained in the ideals, the foundations of the country. Robert Collier once said, "Success is the sum of small efforts repeated day in and day out." That is exactly what I did. Day in and day out. That and ignoring all the commercials that told me I deserve this and the other.

I consider myself fortunate to have experienced living in two very different continents. Love brought me here and the weather kept me frozen. Fargo is home. I had never lived anywhere else other than the country of my birth. I feel richly blessed to have grown up where I did. I am rooted in faith, woven with love, and wrapped with kindness. I feel proud to be American, where I am free to realize my potential and soar to great heights, to be in a place that gives you space to stretch and grow. And that rings true to many young scholars who call America home. I love how America encapsulates the coming together of people from many different nations with stripes of many colors, a patchwork of incredible people. I am happy to just mix in the beauty of my own rainbow.

What lay before your eyes, as you leaf through the pages of this unique book, are the firsthand accounts of brave, enduring, and inspirational journeys. A buffet of "coming to America" stories from all cultures, experiences, and walks of life. A journey that transports you to many corners of the world to experience a kaleidoscope of cultures with a multitude of languages.

In this book are stories laden with enormous hope and dreams of many colors. The painstaking process of tackling the unknown and growing with each small successive effort, as that place where they once laughed and cried and where everybody knew their name becomes but a vivid memory. I invite you to enjoy your first-class experience to these incredible stories of grace, resilience, faith, and hope.

Betty Gronneberg

Founder and executive director of uCodeGirl and author of *The Alphabet Takes a Journey: Destination Ethiopia*

Acknowledgments

First and foremost, this book would not be possible without the thirty student authors from Fargo South High School. Their courage inspires us all; they are the heart and soul of this work. Through their efforts, we are able to transcend boundaries and learn about the truth of the human experience. We are honored to share their words in these pages.

The story of this book begins with Leah Juelke, an EL teacher from South High School in Fargo, ND. After Green Card Voices (GCV) published its first book in Minneapolis, Minnesota, Leah contacted executive director Tea Rozman Clark (at Kevin Brooks's recommendation) about doing a similar book project with students from Fargo South High School. Over the past two years, North Dakota has taken in more refugees per capita than any other US state. The diversity of Fargo specifically is growing quickly; thus we knew partnering with Leah and expanding to Fargo was a good choice. The Bush Foundation agreed and fully funded the project, and *Green Card Youth Voices: Immigration Stories from a Fargo High School* was born.

There have been several people who were absolutely critical to the book's success. Leah Juelke has been our on-the-ground advocate, working with the students tirelessly to bring forth the essays found in this book. Her dedication to her students, her profound enthusiasm as their teacher, and her previous work with their stories has been foundational. Before approaching GCV, Leah had already published smaller scale collections of her students' narratives in *On Second Thought*, a publication of the North Dakota Humanities Council in 2016, and in a self-published volume *Journey to America: Narrative Short Stories* in 2015. These greatly contributed to *Green Card Youth Voices*.

In addtion to Leah, students Samantha Hamernick and Peter Chen of North Dakota State University worked one-on-one with the thirty student authors to turn their spoken words into polished essays. Kevin Brooks has been important for the implementation and support for this project. His community leadership positions in Fargo have been invaluable in helping to spread the word about the book.

Many thanks go to Todd Bertsch, the principal of Fargo South High School, who has supported the project from the moment it popped into Leah

Juelke's mind. Also at Fargo South High School, we would like to thank English and performing arts teacher Kevin Kennedy who provided the space for our recordings.

Critical to this project were Tara Kennedy and Katie Murphy-Olsen. These EL teachers from Wellstone International High School were instrumental in publishing the Minneapolis book and thus were amazing advisors for the Fargo project. Thank you for traveling to Fargo to pass along your expertise!

We contracted with Intermedia Arts's Media Active to do the video recordings. They traveled with us to Fargo and were in our makeshift studio for four days of recording! We especially want to thank Ahxuen Ybarra and Deaundre Dent, who did the videography and photography, as well as Michael Hay for supervision.

Fargo residents, and their neighbors in Moorhead, truly stepped up to the challenge to help make this book come to life.

We could not have made this book happen without the welcoming support of the greater Fargo community: specifically Jessica Thomasson and Shirley Dykshoorn from Lutheran Social Services of North Dakota, who immediately embraced the book idea and made sure we gave voice to the unaccompanied minors who are a part of the project. They also proposed that we launch the book during the annual Building Bridges Conference, the biggest statewide conference pertaining to a wide array of immigrant/refugee issues.

We are so pleased to have the participation of Betty Gronneberg, a first-generation immigrant from Ethiopia. As an immigrant, local Fargo author, Bush Fellow, and executive director of the nonprofit uCodeGirl, Betty was an obvious choice for our foreword author. Her beautiful words are an inspiration for the young immigrants in these pages.

To the media contributors who saw the value in this work and spread the word through their publications, thank you! Specifically we would like to thank Helmut Schmidt of the *Forum of Fargo-Moorhead*, Lisa Farnham of Fargo Public Schools, and Brittney Goodman of the *High Plains Reader*.

To Molly Hill and Amy Bakke, who put in many hours turning the auditory words into written transcripts. Their generosity in committing hours and hours of their time and empathy to these heart-wrenching stories, told with a huge variety of accents, cannot be understated.

Special thanks goes to students of the University of Minnesota's Humphrey School of Public Affairs and Tea Rozman Clark's classroom peers

Barrett Chrissis, John Freude, and Katelynn Rolfes for helping Green Card Voices envision how to develop a strategy to successfully scale our efforts to Fargo.

All this would not be possible without the funding received from the Bush Foundation. Our gratitude goes to Kayla Yang-Best, director of the education portfolio, who saw the value of this project proceeding in Fargo. Thank you for trusting our young nonprofit to be able to successfully replicate the Minneapolis book in North Dakota.

Thanks to the Green Card Voices's board and staff for overseeing the project. Thank you to Tea Rozman Clark, who interviewed all thirty student authors, guided the project, and provided the necessary leadership for this book to realize its fullest potential. Her guidance and commitment to the vision of Green Card Voices continues to motivate everyone she meets. Thank you to José Guzmán, Green Card Voices's graphic designer and video editor, for compellingly presenting these stories and for all your work making moving video narratives. Thank you to Rachel Mueller, the managing editor of the project, who coordinated our efforts, assisted in building community partnerships, and was fundamental to the success of this project. A tremendous thank-you goes to Dara Beevas and our copy editor Patrick Maloney at Wise Ink Creative Publishing for their advice, support, and encouragement. Our collaboration as well as their donations of time and consultation through the InkPossible program greatly enhanced the final product.

Thank you to Veronica Quillien, who designed the study guide and who is also the lead author of *Voices of Immigrant Storytellers: Teaching Guide for Middle and High Schools.* She is a PhD student in the Department of Curriculum and Instruction at the University of Minnesota, and a first-generation immigrant herself. We thank her for her expertise.

There are many individuals who have been critical to the creation of this book and many more who have shown unwavering support. Our work has thrived due to their tremendous encouragement and support. We would like to thank our Green Card Voices board members present—Jessica Cordova Kramer, Johan Eriksson, Faraaz Mohammed, Katie Murphy-Olsen, Masami Suga, George C. Maxwell, Hibo Abdi, Tara Kennedy, Veronica Quillien, and Matt Kim—and past—Miguel Ramos, Jane Graupman, Ali Alizadeh, Laura Danielson, Jeff Corn, Ruhel Islam, Angela Eifert, Kathy Seipp— and all others who have helped our mission along the way.

Introduction

Communities across the United States are ever changing and transforming, although some change faster than others. People have always changed, just as new ideas and innovations replaced the horse and buggy with the automobile. The United States is a nation of immigrants; everyone who is not a Native American or first-generation immigrant is descended from someone who immigrated to these shores by choice or by force. Immigrants bring new ideas and perspectives that enrich us all. They are entrepreneurial, founding new businesses and creating new jobs.

The American landscape is multiracial, multiethnic, and multicultural, which is an inherent strength. An estimated 13.3 percent of our population, or 42.3 million people, were not born in the United States, and immigration to the US is increasing. By 2050, one in five Americans will be an immigrant. This is not unusual, as the United States has enjoyed similar periods in its growth and development. This pattern of immigration has driven our success as immigrants have strengthened the United States for centuries. With these current dramatic and exciting demographic shifts have come challenges and opportunities. Now more than ever, Green Card Voices and other organizations that help share the stories of immigrants have a role to play in expanding our understanding of the immigrant experience and highlighting the countless ways they contribute. To uphold our country's founding principles of justice, equality, and dignity for all, we must remember that with diverse newcomers come growth and innovation. Young new Americans in particular have so much to teach us and so much to share, as you will see within this book.

We believe sharing stories is a powerful tool that can help us reach the goal of a fully integrated and compassionate society. Stories not only empower the teller, whose life experiences and unique contributions become valuable and validated through sharing, but also educate the broader public and help us see how we all share the experience of being human.

Green Card Voices was established as an immigrant storytelling platform, and as we enter into our fourth year, we continue to develop in both our capacity and engagement. Our online videos currently represent 230 voices of people coming from ninety-five countries who now reside in six states.

They are free to watch and are used widely by individuals, schools, community groups, and religious organizations. Our multiple traveling exhibits create physical spaces where the immigrant journey is highly visible and accessible to the public. Our teaching guides help teachers instruct students in classrooms. Last year we launched our latest—and most successful—project: an anthology of books written by diverse youth immigrants.

Our first book, *Green Card Youth Voices: Immigration Stories from a Minneapolis High School* was published in May 2016 with resounding success. The thirty stories in the book were written by first-generation immigrant high school students coming from thirteen different countries. The book won a national award and sold more than 1,500 copies in the first five months. It is being taught at schools around Minneapolis and is required reading at several universities. Because the Minneapolis book has had such a wide impact, we were eager to replicate this model in Fargo, North Dakota, after being invited to do a similar project there.

Though initially quite popular in urban centers, our resources are in higher demand in small towns where they are used by local government organizations, in suburban high schools and libraries, and at community events. The impact of our work in these small towns is even more valuable as it is often the first alternative storytelling media in the region that highlights voices of first-generation immigrants. Representing characteristics of small town America and of a new city center, Fargo became the next ideal city to expand our programming.

With 118,523 residents, Fargo is the largest and most vibrant city in the state of North Dakota. It also has the largest immigration growth per capita in the nation, according to the 2015 US Census. Within the city of Fargo alone, 7.5 percent of the population is foreign-born, over twice that of the state of North Dakota with a 3.2 percent foreign-born population. Most significantly, immigrants are continuing to move to Fargo in growing numbers, with 28.2 percent of immigrants having arrived since 2010. While this new immigrant gateway city is familiar with some anti-immigrant backlash, it is also home to some of the most amazing and innovative work that welcomes immigrants. Truly, the community work that has emerged in recent years is awe-inspiring. The next chapter of the US immigration story is being written in places like Fargo.

Green Card Youth Voices: Immigration Stories from a Fargo High School is one attempt to shift our focus onto the individuals who bring the wisdom of diversity to the fabric of America. At Fargo South High School, about 150 of the 989 students are first-generation immigrants, coming from over twenty-five countries, each with a unique perspective (13 percent of the students in Fargo are foreign-born students). The process of creating this book was specifically designed to meet the needs of the students. One of the important factors we considered was that the majority of the foreign born students at Fargo South High School are SLIFE: Students with Limited or Interrupted Formal Education. As parts of the world experience extreme violence, the opportunity to have consistent quality education is becoming more and more of a privilege. This new reality requires a new approach. Many of the students we talked with work best in "oral mode". For this reason, we recorded the students speaking their stories before we ever approached the page. Using the transcripts from their interviews, their teacher Leah Juelke and volunteers worked with each student to develop their oral stories into polished written essays.

These young people have learned multitudes of languages, played soccer around the world, and worked in restaurants. Their stories show how we all can relate to the joys and growing pains of adolescence. These young people have also suffered kidnapping, split families, illnesses, and loss, but with these trials come tremendous resilience and hope.

Through the process of publishing the book and the subsequent book readings to follow, we hope that these new Americans will be powerful participants and leaders in creating a more vibrant, just, and welcoming democracy for us all. We hope this book will inspire solidarity with, and celebration of, immigrant and refugee contributions. This project will provide a unique opportunity for a variety of community members to engage with people from diverse backgrounds and cultures, thus creating a dynamically connected community.

We began working with the thirty students from Fargo South High School in September of 2016, during one of the most divisive presidential election campaigns in history. Many see the rhetoric of the current administration as unapologetically anti-immigrant and anti-refugee. This book will be published during Donald Trump's first one hundred days in office. It has been exceedingly challenging to work on this book as immigrant, Muslim, and refugee friends have become targets of unwarranted hurtful attacks, based on inaccurate information and an uncharitable, selfish worldview. Yet we knew the critical value of this work. Situated squarely within the crosshairs of the immigration debate are individuals like the students in this book, whose daily lives must continue despite whatever rhetoric dominates our media, our politics, or our dinner table conversations. It is likely that after the 2016 elections, the political reality of how America treats its immigrants will shift dramatically, affecting millions of lives. It is easy to forget how severe the impact can be in the abstract without putting faces, names, and stories to those individuals who will be most directly impacted.

It has been said that a person's story is a window to their soul. Having seen these thirty, we hope you will be moved as we are. We hope you are moved to see that these stories and these people strengthen us, as past immigrants have strengthened us. Their stories demonstrate that they share elements with past immigrants who came seeking a place where they could breathe the free air, live life with dignity, and enjoy equal justice under the law.

The stories you hold in your hands are one remedy; they are the memories, realities, and hopes of thirty young people who, by the turning of countless events, have been brought together in Fargo, North Dakota, from twenty-two countries around the world. In a time when the fabric of the United States is shifting, the magnitude of what we can learn from these youths is incalculable.

The youth of America are the future of America. Based on the resilience, bravery, and courage that the next generation carries, we are in good hands. However, we must continue to create communities of empathy and connectedness in order to keep all of our community members safe, thriving, and contributing. Our sincerest hope is that the courage of these young people inspires us all to actively build a world of compassion and hope.

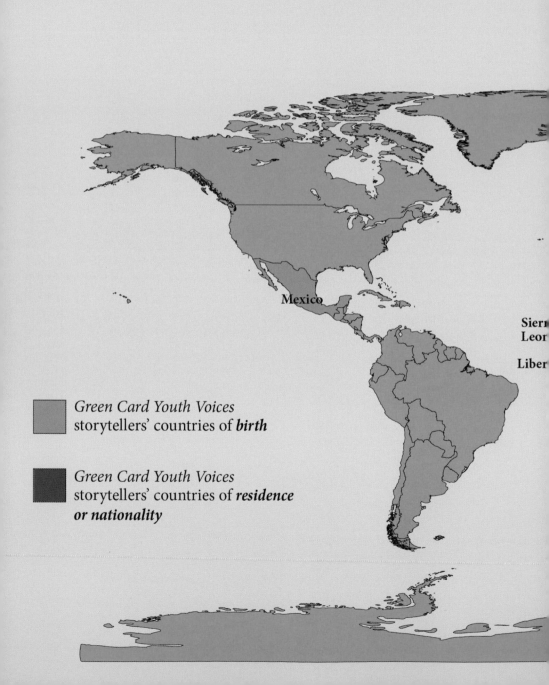

Mexico

Sierr
Leon

Liber

Green Card Youth Voices
storytellers' countries of *birth*

Green Card Youth Voices
storytellers' countries of *residence
or nationality*

World Map

Iraq

Egypt

Chad Sudan Eritrea

Nigeria Ethiopia

Côte Togo Somalia
Ivoire Kenya
Cameroon Uganda

Democratic Tanzania
Republic of the
Congo Zambia

Namibia Burundi Rwanda

Bhutan China

Nepal

Vietnam

Burma
(Myanmar)

Malaysia

Personal Essays

Nyala, Sudàn

Muhend Abakar

From: Nyala, Sudan
Current City: Fargo, ND

> "THERE ARE PEOPLE AROUND THAT WANT TO HELP YOU; THEY'RE GONNA HELP YOU IF YOU ASK. NOBODY WILL HELP IF YOU DON'T ASK FOR IT. "

I was born in Nyala, Sudan. Life there was fine. I still remember the culture and traditions. Life for me wasn't as bad as you'd think because I was young. I didn't know what was going on and I got everything handed to me since I lived with my parents, grandpa, and basically my whole family. I left Sudan when I was around four. I went to Egypt and lived there for most of my life until 2012. That's when I moved here to the US.

I have two brothers and one sister, and one brother was born here in the US. The other one was born in Egypt.

Life in Egypt was weird for me because I was new. In Sudan, there were only Black people, but in Egypt, there was a mixture different races and cultures. I was kind of curious as a kid but then, when I grew up, I began to accept the different cultures around me. When you are in a place with different cultures, your mind opens more and you have to experience stuff to see the differences, which teaches you valuable lessons. That's what fueled my curiosity. If I didn't know something, I had to go further and explore more about it.

In Egypt, there was both good and bad. At first, people were racist. They called me names and stuff like that. But as I got to know people better, I became friends with them, so they began to accept me. Once that happened, we became best friends because we played soccer. In Egypt, a lot of people play soccer on the streets, so we would just get there and ask to join. If you're good, they want to get to know you better and they forget about the negative thoughts they had in mind, and you feel better about yourself.

Life wasn't that difficult in Egypt because I had relatives that lived elsewhere in Europe and America, and because of that, they were able to support us. They sent us money so we wouldn't struggle there. We moved

1

to Egypt because my uncle wanted to help us get a better life. My father quit school early on and got a job to support his brothers and his sisters, and now my uncle wanted to return the favor. My uncle said to my father, "Okay, since you helped me out to finish my education when I was a kid, now I'm going to bring you and your family to Egypt to have a better life."

It was kind of hard for my dad to leave my grandfather because my dad has been by his side since he was born. All of a sudden, he had to leave him for a long time. When we moved to Egypt, life wasn't difficult. Of course, it was that way because of my uncle's support. After around five or six years, my uncle went to Canada. Life for him was better, since Canada was a more developed country. When he got to Canada, he started working and sending money back to Egypt. The Canadian dollar is more valuable than the Egyptian pound, so life wasn't that difficult, but still there was a struggle. There's always struggle no matter where you go in life.

In Darfur, there was a war. People came from places just to pillage. If you had money, they took it away from you. If you had cars or anything of value, they took it away from you. They usually rode camels or horses. If you ran away from them, they had people and roadblocks to stop you. They had weapons, so no matter what you tried to do, they would stop you and just shoot you. The best option for survival was to stop and give them whatever they wanted.

I remember my mom was talking about leaving Egypt. She told us that school was over and we were going to America. I just looked at her and didn't believe it because my parents told me the same thing a year before and it never happened. I still didn't believe them until we started doing the required paperwork. That was when I realized they were actually serious. I was happy and sad at the same time because I was leaving the people that I had grown up with my entire life. I was leaving them, going to a different place with a different culture. I thought it was crazy. I was sad and depressed on the inside because it was just so crazy to leave behind all my friends and family.

My friends came with me to the airport to say good-bye. I kind of wanted to go hide somewhere so I wouldn't have had to go. I remember I gave my friend five Egyptian pounds so he could remember me. I took some pictures from them so I could remember them. Once I got on the airplane, I was looking down at my friends, trying to wave at them, but I couldn't see anything. It was dark outside, so I felt like I was dreaming. It was as if you were watching a romantic or sad movie where one person is leaving the other one behind. I felt like I was going to cry. I did cry, but only on the inside.

In America, I saw people playing soccer, and I was kind of surprised. I thought American people didn't play soccer. I went near them, and inside me, I was kind of nervous to talk to them. Should I go play with them or just stay here and watch them? I stayed because I didn't know them. I didn't speak English well enough to ask people to play.

Then, while I was just standing there, a person came. He was like, "Wanna play with us?" and I was like, "Yeah, sure." I was excited and happy. I was happy that I'd made a new friend in America. When I was playing they were like, "Oh wow, you're pretty good. You should come and play with us every day." From there I started playing with them every day. And that's how I made friends. It was easier to make friends through sports.

If you ask people around the school here, they'll say, "Oh, Muhend, he does every single sport." If you name any sport, I'll tell you that I do it. A lot of people know me through sports because they see me everywhere. Even from different schools, they know my name.

When I first moved, I went to middle school my first year. In Egypt, school didn't look like this. They give you like electronic tablets to use here, not chalkboards. I was surprised. In school you have a desk and you sit by yourself. But in Egypt, you have a whole desk, just like a lunch table, and three or four people sit together. In class, you have like eighty-three, eighty-four people. But here, you have like twenty-three. I was like, "Wow! Why are they wasting all that space here? They could add more desks and put more people in one class and have more people from different places come study there." But, in Egypt, there are eighty-four people just sitting there, and you don't have space to walk around.

Here they have books, books everywhere, and computers in the back. I was like, "Wow, those people really wasted their money on some stupid stuff." But if you really look at it, it's not stupid. It's a good way to get the new Americans to learn. If you don't know something, teachers will actually try to explain it to you. Even if you look at it and you don't understand it, they'll go to computer and show it to you on Google. They'll translate it for you. They'll find a way to teach you.

In Egypt, if you don't know something, you don't know it. You find your own way to learn it. Teachers don't care about you. They just want you to come to school; they take the money and go home. They do the same thing over and over. But here, they don't even think about money. They just wanna find the best way, the easiest way to teach you. And it actually works. They're also nice people when they teach.

Teachers here don't hit you. In Egypt, if you come late to class, you get whipped. If you don't do your homework, get ready to get whipped. If two or three people are talking in class and the teacher gets mad, they'll tell everyone to stand up and start hitting the whole class. You open your hands, and the teacher hits you with a long stick. And sometimes they tell you to turn around and just whip your butt with it. But here, you can say whatever you want to the teachers and they don't do anything to you. They will come talk to you, tell you to respect yourself and stuff like that or maybe send you to the office. The office doesn't do anything.

My friend Minka encouraged me to do basketball. We had basketball in Egypt, but nobody played it. They actually tried to make me play it, and I was like, "You must be crazy." Then I saw a lot of people going there and joining the team, and I was like, "Okay, I'm gonna go with them." Minka was one of my first friends, I guess.

I didn't know how to dribble a ball. I just did some stuff that I made up. People laughed because they thought it was weird. I saw the half court and I went to shoot from there because I thought it was the three-point line. Then I went to the three-point line and I was like, "If I shoot from here it'll just be two points, so I should go shoot from the half line to get three points." People just laughed at me, and then they started making fun of me. I didn't like it. I was like, "Okay, maybe I should try to improve myself." I tried to train, but I didn't know how to train because I didn't have a coach to train me well during the summer time.

Then track season came. I joined track. I played soccer, so I could run. I beat people and some people beat me. I was like, "I can't let this kid beat me. He looks younger than me. He's shorter than me. I can beat him." I tried to train harder and harder. It was still not working because I was not training right. By the time I got faster, track season was over. When I got to high school, I felt like I could do track and be better at it because I tried to prepare myself to reach my goal. And then I just started running. I was like, "I know I can beat this person, I can beat you."

People didn't believe it. They were like, "Last year, you didn't go anywhere. You were the slowest one on our team." People were putting me down until the race started and I proved them wrong. They were like, "Oh, wow, I didn't know you could run." From there, people started getting closer to me.

If you are successful, people come closer to you. That motivates me to work harder and harder to make people come closer to me.

I started joining sports to make more friends and be like normal people here. To have friends here, you talk to him, you talk to him, you talk to her. You have best friends. I guess I didn't have best friends, and I had to find a way to get friends to be my best friends.

In the future I want to be a computer engineer. My uncle back in Egypt used to like fixing computers. He was pretty good at it, but he wouldn't let me come close to him. In his mind, it was a distraction. Back then, when people were working, they didn't want little kids to be close to them. I wanted to learn and to see the stuff he was doing. Whenever I went close to him, he'd be like, "Get out of here, go there, go there, do this." He tried to find something distracting for me to do to make me go away. I was like, "One day, I'm gonna get older and do the same thing you're doing, and even better." That's the reason I want to be a computer engineer.

At the same time, I kind of don't like it. I went for a job shadow and I saw people sitting by a computer and just typing and sitting by themselves. I didn't like that, because I like working with people. I like working as a team. That's the part that I don't like. But still, I want to go to reach my goal that I set seven or ten years ago. That is probably going to be my future job, I guess.

My advice to new Americans would be don't be shy to ask for help. I know it's hard to ask for help in class because you're surrounded by different people and your culture is different from theirs. It's hard for you to say or do the stuff you wanna do because there are people around you who will laugh at you. You just get nervous like, "Oh my god, no, I'm not going to do this." No, just do whatever you feel is right. Do what you wanna do; ask for help.

There are people around that want to help you; they're gonna help you if you ask. Nobody will help if you don't ask for it. They don't know what you need. Explain your story so they know where you came from.

greencardvoices.org/speakers/muhend-abakar

N'Djamena, Chad

Ruth Mekoulom

From: N'Djamena, Chad
Current City: Fargo, ND

"MY INTERPRETERS ARE BEAUTIFUL! MY LANGUAGE IS BEAUTIFUL! I LOVE AMERICAN SIGN LANGUAGE AND LEARNING. I WANT TO LEARN FOREVER."

I was born in Chad, and I'm seventeen years old. My family includes my mom, Sara; my brothers, Regit and Abakar; and my sister, Prisca. My dad is still in Africa.

When I was five, I was living in Chad and became very sick. I also became a big sister to Prisca. I remember not wanting to hold my sister because I was sick. My parents noticed that I was not responding to my name. They would yell and look for me, but I wouldn't come. They realized that I'd become deaf from my illness, but there was no place in Chad that could help me. There was also a war happening in our country. My parents became worried, so we moved to Cameroon. I grew up there until I was thirteen.

When we arrived in Cameroon, my parents took me to a doctor to check my hearing. The doctor told my mom about a school for the deaf. At first, I was very nervous to start school. I didn't understand sign language. I learned to sign and write. I had some friends there, but later I was bullied. I wanted to quit school, but Mom wanted me to have a good education. I didn't get to school very often, and I was always late coming home at night. I would ride the bus early in the morning and then ride the bus home. I went to school for two years. Then I had to quit at age eleven because it was too expensive. So my mom started asking about who could help us move to America.

I remember my mom buying many new clothes and noticing that she was packing. I asked why she was packing, and she told me we were moving to America. She was very excited, but I was not so sure. I didn't want to move to America; I wanted to stay in Africa because I had a lot of friends there.

Suddenly, I was going to many doctor appointments and having pictures taken. I was fingerprinted and had lots of shots. On March 17, 2013, we finally came to America. It was my first flight. We flew to France, then to Chicago, before finally arriving in Fargo. It was a long flight. In all, we had ten people in my family move here. I was very nervous on the plane, but the flights were smooth. I was very afraid of the escalators in the airports. I didn't want to ride them, but I had to.

That was the first time I saw snow. I remember asking my mom what that white stuff was, and she didn't know. When we arrived in Fargo, I hated the snow. It was very cold. There was a woman who met us at the airport. She was a French interpreter, and she was there with a couple of white ladies. They drove us to our new home, an apartment in West Fargo. They showed us how everything worked in the kitchen, bedrooms, and bathroom. The ladies left, and we were alone for the night. I went into my bedroom and thought, "This is so different from Africa. Not similar at all." There was a refrigerator, and there was a kind of food that we didn't have in Africa. We were nervous for our new life in America and sad because we had left twenty people in Africa. Hopefully they will come soon.

The next day, the ladies came back and gave us some money. We went to the doctor for shots. The same ladies helped our family for six months.

I started going to school when I was thirteen or fourteen at West Fargo. My mom walked with me in the school for a tour. Everyone spoke. There was no sign language. I didn't understand what people were saying. There was a woman who spoke French who helped me. I had a new teacher, Carla, who taught me math, science, and the alphabet in sign language. She made me change to English words. School was tough. People thought I was lazy.

I felt frustrated because nobody understood me. I felt lonely. Communication was my barrier. I had no clue what was going on. I was the only deaf student there, and everyone else was speaking. Only one person tried to communicate with me.

My mom also started going to school to learn English. At that time she didn't have a job yet. She was just working on her English before she got a job.

I received a hearing evaluation and hearing aids for the first time. I still didn't understand or like the hearing aids. My mom decided to take me to Minneapolis for surgery. We spent the night in Minneapolis. I was put to sleep and there was a surgery done to put in a cochlear implant. I was in so much pain. Mom asked me if I wanted to stay or go home, but I didn't understand what was going on. I had a hard time walking. My cochlear implant was activated, and it scared me. I could hear beeps. I didn't like it. We tried auditory training but I still didn't understand. I still don't like hearing aids or my cochlear implant, so I do not wear them.

In April of 2014, our family moved to Fargo and I started at South High School. It was the first time I met my teacher, Baml, who is a teacher for the deaf and hard of hearing, and she signs just like I do. My signs were very limited, and she worked hard to teach me many words. There was another deaf student who signed, Sumaili, at South High School. He signed much faster than me. This helped me learn so much. Now, I can sign fast and use many words. I can take classes and understand. I have sign language interpreters who help me understand what is said in class. My interpreters are beautiful! My language is beautiful! I love American Sign Language and learning. I want to learn forever.

I spoke French before I lost my hearing. My family still communicates with me in French. I have to rely on lipreading in French because my family does not sign. I am teaching my family American Sign Language so they can communicate with me.

When school is done I like to play soccer with friends. I like to go shopping, hang out with the girls, paint nails, and braid hair. My new hobby is sewing sewing skirts and dresses. Also for fun I like to play games and hang out. I'd like to work in a spa someday. I'd like to give massages to people, do their hair, do their makeup, and paint their nails. I also want to work as a missionary and sew clothes.

Now my life is so much better. I have a lot of friends at South High School. I miss Africa but Fargo is my home.

greencardvoices.org/speakers/ruth-mekoulom

Jhapa, Nepal

Pal Gurung

From: Jhapa, Nepal
Current City: Fargo, ND

"MY FAMILY WAS NERVOUS ABOUT BEING IN A NEW COUNTRY, BUT THAT NERVOUSNESS QUICKLY TURNED TO JOY WHEN WE FINALLY REUNITED WITH OUR RELATIVES AFTER BEING APART FOR SO MANY YEARS."

My name is Pal Gurung, and I was born in Jhapa, Nepal, in the Timai refugee camp. We lived in the refugee camp because my parents were part of a group of minorities in Bhutan who faced government persecution. They fled to the refugee camp along with millions of others and got married in the refugee camp.

My life in camp was difficult. Often times we didn't have enough supplies or enough food to eat. We were always thankful to the UN because they provided us with food, clothes, and even an education. Our home was made up of bamboo, and it was rather cramped. We had to share the kitchen and bedroom with other families and our bathroom was a communal bathroom outside. Waking up early, going to school, coming back home to help with chores, and preparing for school the next day was a stressful life, and that is how my life was for fourteen years.

One night, we were eating dinner with other families, and my father told us we were going to apply to go to the US. Thus, we filled out the forms, went through interviews, got medical checks, etc. After a while we were finally approved. We were nervous and scared when we got our approval because we were scared to go to a country with a totally different language and culture. We were also super sad to leave our family, especially our grandma, who had to stay in Nepal with our uncle. Despite our best attempts to persuade her, she decided to stay in Nepal.

After we were approved, we had to go through orientation. At orientation, they taught us ways to adjust to life in America, such as how to use the bathroom, how to shop, how to speak the language, as well as how to make a 911 call in case of emergency. When orientation was over, we went back and waited until IOM gave us a call telling us the exact date of our departure.

I don't really remember that much about our journey. I remember that we took a plane to New York, then to Chicago, then to Fargo. I was scared because it was my first time on a plane. The food on the plane wasn't that great, but I ate it anyways because I was so hungry. It was also confusing navigating the airplane for when we had to use the bathroom or asking people to move aside when we had to go out and stretch our bodies.

When we arrived in Fargo, my uncles and cousins were waiting for us. My family was nervous about being in a new country, but that nervousness quickly turned to joy when we finally reunited with our relatives after being apart for so many years. They took us to their home because we did not have a home yet.

After one month, I started school. My first day in the school was difficult, and I was nervous because I did not know much English. But as time went on, things became much clearer and I was finally starting to adapt.

My family is happy here in the US now. I have one older sister and now a younger sister as well. I love to play guitar and sing my cultural songs. I want to play soccer for Fargo South and become a software engineer in the future.

greencardvoices.org/speakers/pal-gurung

Bukavu, Democratic
Republic of the Congo

Nakafu Kahasha

From: Bukavu, Democratic Republic of the Congo
Current City: Fargo, ND

"YOU JUST BE YOU. NO MATTER WHAT, THEY'RE NOT GOING TO CHANGE YOU. "

I lived in Congo with my mom, dad, and sisters. I don't remember everything, but I remember hearing gunshots when I was little. We didn't even know where they came from. My parents told everybody to hide under the bed, so we did. They told us that we better leave and find a safe place. So we went to Tanzania. We stayed there for about three weeks, and then my siblings and I went to a refugee camp. My parents didn't go. They went to Congo to be with my grandparents because they were sick. I never saw my parents again.

We had a little money, and in Africa, when you have money, people are desperate and try to kill you for it. My uncle called us and told us someone was coming to kill us, so we decided to run away to another refugee camp.

My life was terrible. When I came to the refugee camp, it only had one kind of food, and it was green beans. I don't know if I was allergic, but I kept getting sick. The first time I got sick was when I was seven years old. My brothers didn't know what was happening. I kept sweating and my whole body was shaking. The ambulance took me to a different city. I was all by myself. My brother knew a lady that was willing to take care of me. I stayed with her a while, and she spoke English. Soon I had to move to a different camp, so I couldn't stay with her anymore. I thought I'd feel better, but I got sick again. I ended up having malaria, and some of the medicine made my whole body itch.

When we were in the refugee camp, we couldn't call anyone. We had to go to the forest to find food. We had to walk miles to get water. In Africa, when you are an eight-year-old girl, you know how to do a lot of stuff. You quickly learn how to cook and take care of your siblings.

15

One day, the process started for us to go to another country. They asked us a lot of questions. They didn't question me because I was little, but they questioned my two brothers and my sister-in-law. After one month, they put our names on the board, and then a lady told us we were going to America. I was so happy.

When I got to Fargo, I thought it was a beautiful place but nothing like home in Africa. I wished that my parents were there so we could've shared those moments together. It was me, my brothers, my sister-in-law, and my twin nieces. It was really freezing, not like the weather in Africa.

Our caseworker picked us up at the airport and took us home. We just smiled because English was hard for us. When he talked, we only smiled. When he smiled, we smiled back. When I got here, I thought the clothes were ugly. I don't like to wear sweaters or jackets or mittens.

I didn't like the food either. In the fridge, there were different kinds of vegetables. I don't eat vegetables, milk, or cheese. Why should I eat vegetables? I'm not a dog or a cow. So we only cooked African food, and my brother would go to the African market.

It was summer when we arrived, so we went to summer school. I took a test and they put me in fifth grade because I was good at math and reading. For summer school, I had to ride the bus. I didn't know where to go so my brother took me to the bus everyday and picked me up so I wouldn't get lost.

The thing I like about high school is people don't care what anyone thinks of them. They don't care what people say about them. You just be you. No matter what, they're not going to change you. The other thing I like about high school is that a lot of people are friendly and kind.

Freshman year I played soccer and volleyball, and sophomore year I played soccer. I really like playing soccer because I love to run around. I want to be in dance class, but they don't have the kind of dance class I like. They only have ballet. I like hip-hop. But I like soccer because you get to know a lot of people. You get to have friends to talk to. It's just fun. If you are mad and you go to soccer everything will be good in your brain. You'll be just thinking about soccer and just playing with your friends. It's a fun sport to do.

Last year, my teacher Mrs. Juelke made us write a story about how we came to the US. At first, I hated the idea. I wanted to write it, but it was hard. I didn't want to remember the bad times. Then I just started and kept going. I finished before everybody else and my story was actually good. We read it out loud in public. I was scared because it was my first time reading out loud in front of a lot of people. I was so glad that everybody liked my story. Because of her, I became famous, and everybody knows me now. I'm really thankful for her and how she helped me.

I want to become a nurse or a first-grade teacher or a flight attendant. The main reason I want to be a flight attendant is because I want to travel around the world. I want to see how it is, how beautiful it is, and maybe I can get the chance to go back to my country and visit my family and friends who live there because I really miss them.

greencardvoices.org/speakers/nakafu-kahasha

Senafe, Eritrea

Akberet Tewelde

From: Senafe, Eritrea
Current City: Fargo, ND

"AT FIRST, I WAS SO CONFUSED ABOUT THE TIME DIFFERENCE. WHAT TIME WAS MORNING AND WHAT TIME WAS NIGHT? I HAD NO IDEA."

I was born Eritrea, and my life was good. I lived with my family. I went on vacation sometimes. I have three brothers and one sister. I went to middle school with my brother when I lived there. In Eritrea, the weather doesn't change from winter to summer. The weather is so good. When it's winter, it's warm. When it's summer, it's warm. I liked the food in Eritrea. There is this pancake-like bread that we call injera. In my home, they cooked injera every day with soup. During the weekends, I played with my friends, biked, and played soccer.

I left my parents behind in Eritrea because my brothers went to Ethiopia and I wanted to be with them and have a good future. After two years, I went to Ethiopia by myself to join them, but I didn't find my brothers; they had already left to go to Israel. After some time, my older brother came back to Ethiopia. I ended up staying in a small refugee camp for a couple days and then went to a larger camp. There were people to meet me and show me where to go. When I went there, I saw my brother. I lived in a small hut with six girls.

I was in a main camp called Ayni. When you live there, you can go back to the food corridor and bring food home to cook. They have a big river you can go swimming in. Monday through Friday, you go to school. You can go to church on Sunday if you want. On Saturday, you can go play soccer. They have soccer for girls or boys.

They started a process in the camp with lists of names on paper. You can check your name and look at the date for an interview. At the interview, people asked where you were from and how long you have been at the camp. After two weeks, they come back and they put your name on a list. Then, you go to another interview.

I came to the US as an unaccompanied minor because I wasn't with my parents. When my immigration paperwork finished, I flew to Fargo, North Dakota. At the airport, my foster family, case manager, and interpreter were there. At first, I was so confused about the time difference. What time was morning and what time was night? I had no idea. I got put with a foster family, and they showed me a lot and helped me.

Because I didn't speak any English, I didn't understand anything. I started school at the Welcome Center in West Fargo when I first came to Fargo. After a year, I went to the local high school. I liked that better because it was close to my new house. After a year, my older brother came to Fargo from Ethiopia, so I moved in with him and then had to change schools to Fargo South.

My life is good. I miss my family because I haven't seen them for a long time. That's the only problem, but I have good life because I live with my brother and cousin.

When I lived in West Fargo, I worked at a Mexican restaurant. I changed my job and started working at the Chinese restaurant in the mall. At first it was so hard because I didn't know how to be a cashier. I soon learned how to do it and it wasn't so bad.

In the future, I want to go college at North Dakota State University. When I get my degree, I want to go back my country and work there.

---

greencardvoices.org/speakers/akberet-tewelde

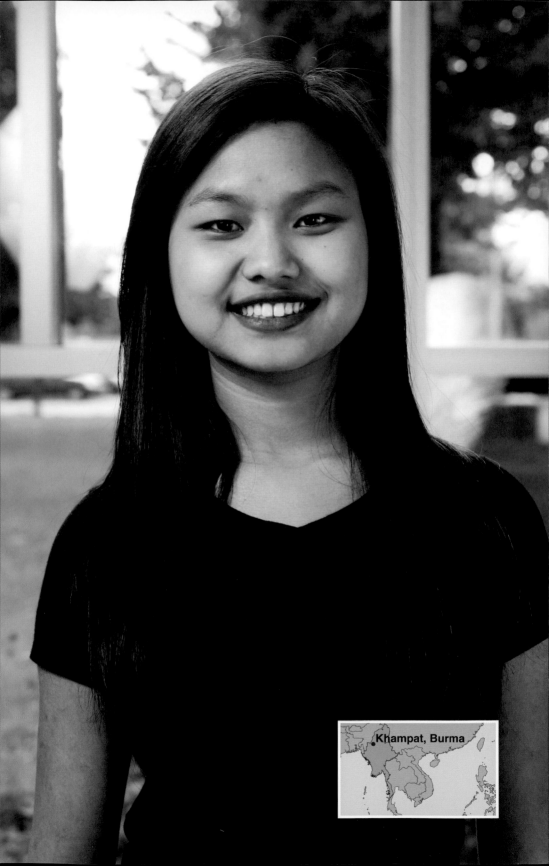

Khampat, Burma

Biak Sung

From: Khampat, Burma
Current City: Fargo, ND

> "SINCE WE GOT HERE IN THE MIDDLE OF WINTER, IT WAS REALLY, REALLY COLD. WHEN I LOOKED OUTSIDE, I SAW NO ONE ON THE STREETS, NOT EVEN AN ANIMAL."

I was born in Khampat, Burma, which is a small town. I'm the youngest of three in my family. When I was three years old, my dad left for Malaysia to get a better job. Around the same time, my brother and my mother passed away. I lived with my grandparents until I was in first grade. I started school, but they had trouble paying my school fees. My grandparents thought it would be better for my sister and me to live in an orphanage because we could at least go to school there. We lived in the orphanage for seven years. The directors were like our mom and dad. I loved them so much.

One day, we heard from my dad. He was planning to apply to go to the US, and he wanted me and my sister to come with him. It was so hard for me to leave my new "parents" at the orphanage. I didn't want to leave and go to America.

Eventually, we joined my dad in a different city, and he brought us to the United States so we could all live together.

I rode on many airplanes. I didn't know how many there were, but there were a lot of them. I was the youngest sibling, and everything was really confusing. I don't remember much about our journey. I can only remember Chicago and Fargo. We were on a big plane when we flew to Chicago and a small plane when we flew to Fargo.

When we first saw my dad, we were very happy. I didn't really know who my dad was or what he looked like because I was only three months old when he left for Malaysia. So fifteen years later, when I saw him for the first time at the Fargo airport, I didn't really know what to expect. But I was happy just to be able to see my dad again.

I cried for two or three days when I first got to Fargo because I felt sad and lonely without my relatives. I especially missed my grandpa and grandma. We didn't have any relatives living here in Fargo. Since we got here in the middle of winter, it was really, really cold. When I looked outside, I saw no one on the streets, not even an animal.

When we first got here, we didn't have a car, so we had to take the bus for simple errands like grocery shopping. We had to wait in the snow for fifteen to thirty minutes, and it was miserable. It was really, really cold. Now, my life is much better compared to when I first got to Fargo. I'm still learning the English language, but I know much more of it now.

I love math. Math is all about problem solving, which is something that I enjoy. Other subjects are kind of hard for me because my English is, despite the improvements, still at a pretty low level. I am involved in Key Club and tennis club, both of which are really fun.

A college prep program called Upward Bound has really helped me prepare for the future. They teach me English, math, and science in the summer to help me better prepare for classes. They also help me with my homework, so when I don't know something or am stuck on a certain problem, I can turn to them for help. I hope to become a cardiologist someday. I want to go into the medical field to help people.

greencardvoices.org/speakers/biak-sung

Jhapa, Nepal

Anjana Chuwan

From: Jhapa, Nepal
Current City: Fargo, ND

> "I STARTED IN FOURTH GRADE BUT THE PEOPLE THERE WERE REALLY RUDE TO ME. THEY MADE FUN OF ME FOR WHAT I WORE AND HOW I SPOKE. SINCE I DIDN'T KNOW THAT MUCH ENGLISH, THEY WERE REALLY SCARED TO BE FRIENDS WITH ME."

My parents were born in Bhutan. I only know that they got kicked out of Bhutan and they moved to Timai refugee camp in Nepal, where I was born. My mom used to work in a hospital, but I don't really remember where my dad worked. I think he worked in construction.

I don't really remember much about my life back in camp. I remember images of me walking to school with my friends or playing with them. I remember that the house we used to live in was made out of brick and bamboo. I recall that back in school our teachers were rude to us and would beat us if we didn't turn our homework in on time. We had one teacher for each subject, and my favorite was math.

I was eight or nine years old when we moved to the United States. It was my first time on an airplane, and I slept for most of the time. What I remember about that trip the most was walking to the different planes and sleeping basically all day and all night. I am not sure about the name of the cities that we passed through.

On the flight to Idaho, though, I was wearing a pair of pants with a flower on it. One of the old guys who sat next to me on the flight kept trying to pull the flower off. He actually managed to pull the flower off. I got really scared and cried to my mom about it, but she just laughed it off.

I lived in Boise, Idaho, for around three to four years. We arrived on November 1, 2011. It was really cold, but there wasn't that much snow because it technically was still fall. I remember seeing all the different colored leaves on the ground. I started in fourth grade, but the people there were really rude to me. They made fun of me for what I wore and how I spoke. Since I didn't know that much English, they were really scared to be friends with me. My teacher was also really rude. I remember that she would yell at the class almost every single day. I went to classes at a community center where they taught me English and how to use computers and helped me with my homework. If I was stuck on homework, then I would go there for help.

We moved to Fargo in the summer of 2014. We moved here because my mom's parents lived here. I started in seventh grade that following fall. Now I am a freshman in high school. It is better here because all my cousins go to school here and there are other Nepalese students for me to hang out with, some of whom are actually my childhood friends.

My favorite subject in school right now is still math. I'm not sure of what I want to be yet, but many of my friends tell me that I should be a lawyer because I like to talk and argue a lot. I also would kind of like to become a flight attendant. I don't know. We'll see.

greencardvoices.org/speakers/anjana-chuwan

Rucuro, Democratic
Republic of the Congo

Musoni Mudatinya

From: Rucuro, Democratic Republic of the Congo
Current City: Fargo, ND

"SINCE WE WERE UNPREPARED FOR THE FARGO WEATHER, WE COPIED OTHER PEOPLE. IF THEY WORE GLOVES THEN WE WORE GLOVES AND IF THEY WORE JACKETS, THEN WE WORE JACKETS."

I was born in Rucuro, Congo. I lived with my grandparents on a farm. One day, we saw a fire in the sky, and people were shooting around us. My grandpa told us to hide, so we hid in the forest. When the shooting stopped, we went back to our house. My grandpa told us to stay in the house because people were trying to kill us.

Later, we went out to the city center and saw soldiers coming and saying that they won. They told us to go back to our homes, so we went home. My grandpa told my family to move to Rwanda because if we stayed in Congo, the rebels would keep trying to kill us. We then moved to Rwanda on a truck. We sat on top of a bunch of boards in the back. A soldier came out of the forest and asked the driver to stop. The driver didn't stop, so the soldier started shooting at us. We shouted to the driver to stop and he stopped. The soldier then wanted money from the driver, but when he saw one of his captains inside of the truck, he decided to let us pass.

We arrived in Rwanda in 1996. After we got some food and supplies from a main center, they separated the refugees into different camps. They brought my family to the Kiziba Refugee Camp, where we stayed for over fifteen years. Throughout that time, we saw many refugees from Congo who told us that the fighting hadn't stopped. Six months after arriving in camp, we ran out of food, so my grandpa asked the camp directors for some food for us. We waited months to see if we could get enough food. Food was always scarce, and people would beg each other for food.

There were around twenty thousand people in the camp. Some left to go to the US while others took their spot. There were small white houses, but after they ran out of houses they started to use tents. The tents were too small for the six of us, so a few of us, sometimes even three of us, would sleep on one mat.

School was only supported through ninth grade. After that, you would usually wait to see if someone could help you continue school. There were a lot of smart kids, but they didn't have enough money to continue school. Girls were luckier than boys. People from refugee organizations wanted girls to continue their schooling, so they would help some girls who had passed ninth grade to keep going. That did require some money though, so often parents would go out of camp to try and make some money.

Around 2008 or 2009, we started to see the International Organization of Migration. They came inside of the camp and chose some people for an interview. The interview would allow refugees to go to other countries.

When I found out that we were going to America, I was really happy. I was also sad because I was going to leave my friends, but I told myself that maybe I could help some of them get to America as well. My family celebrated and thought of our first time flying, the different types of people we were going to meet, and the fact that we were going to speak English. Even though we didn't know any English yet, we were in a good mood.

We went to Kenya, Belgium, New York, Chicago, and finally Fargo. When I first got to the airport, I was scared because it was my first time on the airplane. My grandma didn't want to get in because she said there was nothing in the sky on which the airplane could stand. We told her it was going to be all right, and she got on the plane. There were many people in the various airplanes who were willing to help us. I didn't like the airplane food, though, so when I arrived in Fargo I hadn't eaten much.

Our caseworker came out to greet us. He took us to our house and showed us how the appliances and other stuff worked. Then we ate. I didn't quite like the chicken though.

The next morning, I saw a black woman, and I was surprised because I had always thought that there were only white people in America. Even my grandma didn't believe that there was a black woman here to see us. Then the woman came into our house and started speaking our language. We were shocked, since we didn't know that there were people in Fargo who could do that. We asked her to show us how the appliances and tools worked again because we couldn't understand the English of our caseworker. We then asked her to show us around Fargo and introduce us to our neighbors.

She took us to various stores, including an African market. We went and bought African ingredients, and she cooked for us. After we ate, people came to visit and welcome us to the United States. When people mentioned snow, I was lost because I didn't know what it was. Since we were unprepared for the Fargo weather, we copied other people. If they wore gloves, we wore gloves. If they wore jackets, we wore jackets. Our caseworker came to our house and took us to buy winter clothes. He told us how to dress so we wouldn't get sick.

After being in our apartment for five months, my uncles and I started school. My two uncles were just a couple years older than I was. We were shy and scared. We were sitting alone because English was hard for us, but we kept trying to talk with people. Sadly, after being in school for a couple months, my uncle passed away while swimming in a pool. My grandma also passed away. Life was very sad and difficult.

My life has changed a lot. I have found a job on my own, and I am doing some stuff by myself now. Life for my family is easier because things are more affordable now. I have already started saving money for my future, including college. School is great. We get to choose the subjects we want to study, and teachers here teach much better than the teachers taught back in my country. I want to study electrical technology in the future. I also hope to go back to Rwanda and visit my friends to see how they are doing after all this time.

greencardvoices.org/speakers/musoni-mudatinya

Tianjin, China

Tristen Hagen

From: Tianjin, China
Current City: Fargo, ND

> "I WAS UPSET THAT I WAS GOING TO HAVE TO LEAVE MY FRIENDS AND MY GIRLFRIEND AND MY GRANDPARENTS. BUT I WAS HAPPY THAT I WAS FINALLY GOING TO BE REUNITED WITH MY DAD."

I was born in Tianjin, China. I lived with my mom, my grandparents, and my younger sister. My dad was in America. My life was pretty good. I went to Chinese school. My hobby was basketball. Because my dad was in America, we used FaceTime, Skype and other forms of social media.

American school is really different from Chinese school. They didn't have any sports in China, and they gave us a lot of homework. I took Math, English, Chinese, PE, History, Biology, and Geography. Math in China is really, really hard. It's way different than America. That's why I'm really good at math right now in American school.

I didn't travel much to other cities in China; I went to Beijing, the capital of China, and Guangzhou. These cities are pretty similar to the city I live in. It's pretty different than an American city, like Fargo.

The day my mom told me we were going to move to America, I was pretty nervous. It was hard. I was upset that I was going to have to leave my friends and my girlfriend and my grandparents. But I was happy that I was finally going to be reunited with my dad.

I packed all my stuff and brought it to the airport. That was the second time I had been to an airport, but the first time was when I was three years old so I couldn't remember it. There were many different people at the airport. There were huge airplanes. My mom was leading us the whole time, and I didn't understand the process. First, we landed in Chicago; it was a different place. We went out to eat in a restaurant. Then we went back to the airport and took a small plane to Fargo.

When I landed in Fargo and got off the plane, I couldn't hear anything in my left ear and I didn't know why, but two hours later, it recovered. My dad and his friend picked us up from the airport. When I saw my dad, I gave him a hug, and I was almost crying because I was so happy. A girl from the neighborhood was telling me, "I'm your friend" in Chinese; this made me happy. She was my first friend in America.

After being in America for about three months, I went to school. It was pretty difficult for me because my English was not that good, but now my English is getting better. I had no friends at that school at first because my only friend went to Moorhead High School. The first sport I started was basketball.

After one year in America, I went to the high school, where I started playing football; my first position was right guard. Before the season started, my dad told me that football was a physical sport and that it would be difficult, but I decide to try it anyway.

The biggest difference coming to America from China was the people; in China, they are all Asian. Since I did not speak any English in China, it was difficult coming to America and having to do everything in English. Because of this, for the first year, I stayed at home and didn't go anywhere. After the first year, I could speak enough English to buy stuff and talk to people.

My goal is to go to NDSU for engineering. Also, I would love to play football for them, so that it what I am practicing for.

---

greencardvoices.org/speakers/tristen-hagen

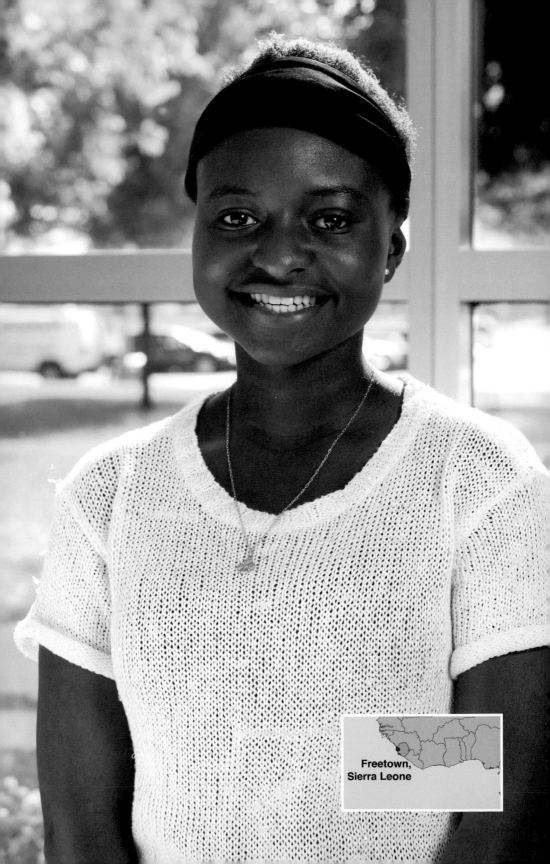

Freetown,
Sierra Leone

Joyce Showers

From: Freetown, Sierra Leone
Current City: Fargo, ND

> "I'VE BEEN HERE FOR TEN YEARS AND THOSE TEN YEARS HAVE BEEN REALLY GOOD FOR ME EDUCATION-WISE. IT HAS MADE ME ABLE TO UNDERSTAND MORE IN LIFE. MY ENGLISH HAS CONSTANTLY IMPROVED AND I FEEL LIKE I AM NOW ABLE TO ACHIEVE SOMETHING FOR MYSELF."

I was born in Freetown, Sierra Leone. What I remember is that every Saturday I used to go to my grandma's house. I hung out with my grandmother and my cousins, and it was nice just being able to be with family. Sierra Leone was really hot. June through September were typical rainy months. It rained a lot and the streets would be flooded with a lot of water. My grandparents lived on a hill to avoid the rain. The rain was overwhelming. There were food vendors on the streets, which was nice.

My family was made up of my father, my mother, my stepsister, younger sister, and me. My stepsister didn't grow up with us; she grew up with my grandmother. My other sister and I grew up with our mom. My stepsister only came to see us on the weekends and when we came to see her. She wasn't really fond of us in the beginning because she wanted all of my grandmother's attention.

My grandparents lived in a middle-class neighborhood, so she received a better education than us. Both her dad as well as my grandparents were teachers, so they taught her a lot of what they knew, including English, something that my other sister and I didn't quite have the luxury of having. Thus, when we came to America, we didn't know any English at all. We were trying to get people to understand us, but that was really difficult, and I guess looking back at it now, it was somewhat humorous. My stepsister knew a little bit of English, and that helped us, which was really nice.

Because I didn't know any English, learning in America was extremely difficult. When I came to America, I started in the first grade. It was a little bit hard because people were really mean. They made fun of me and called me names. I had to move to a different school due to the bullying. The new school was Lincoln Elementary, and it was completely different because everybody was really nice and open-minded. Still though, I was bullied on the school bus because of my voice and my height.

School finally had its breakthrough. I had an EL teacher who taught me English and I was finally able to understand it. I was able to use it and communicate with other people, which was really nice. I didn't like the food, though. The food was really gross. Also, I remember in second grade I went to my mom complaining about how I couldn't understand my teacher because she was talking too fast. My sister wrote in my planner asking the teacher to slow down so that I could understand what she was trying to say. That helped, and in the end I got it.

I've been here for ten years and those ten years have been really good for me education-wise. It has made me able to understand more in life. My English has constantly improved, and I feel like I am now able to achieve something for myself. During those years, it was really nice because my whole family was happily together. We got used to the American customs such as Christmas, Thanksgiving, and Easter.

My mom always cooked turkey. I remember when she cooked turkey for the first time and it wasn't good because she had never done it before. Looking back at it, it was like a nice experiment because now every Thanksgiving we have a tradition of who makes this and who makes that. My sister made the casserole and I made the mashed potatoes and my mom would just stick to the turkey because she's good at that now. We also have a similar thing for Christmas.

High school is nice and I have the opportunity to be involved in many activities. I'm currently a junior and after school I go to debate and student congress, which has helped me with my speaking and my writing. I hope to be able to put that onto my college application so that I can get a good scholarship. I don't really have a favorite subject in school. I would say that I am really great at math and English though.

When I'm older I want to be a nurse practitioner. It has been my dream since I was little. Seeing sick people quite often, I would like to be able to take care of people and help them out.

I also want to share that when we came here, my mom gave birth to my brother. She had always wanted a boy because back at home, relatives were mean to my mom because she had three girls. When she found out, it was totally unexpected and she was really surprised. It almost seemed like a miracle that God had given her, a reward for this journey we have made.

greencardvoices.org/speakers/joyce-showers

Jhapa, Nepal

Badal Mongar

From: Jhapa, Nepal
Current City: Fargo, ND

"IT WAS REALLY TOUGH FOR ME TO LEAVE MY COUNTRY, BUT I WAS EXCITED TO MOVE SOMEWHERE NEW. "

I was born in Nepal. When I was just seven or eight years old, we went to the village to celebrate our festival. There was an argument between the native village people and us, the refugee people. The native people wanted know why the refugees were in their country. They were upset and wanted us to go back to Bhutan. I was born in the refugee camp in Nepal, so I considered Nepal to be my country. Hearing people talk to us like that made me very sad.

I asked my auntie about why they came to Nepal. She explained that my family used to live in Bhutan, but the Bhutanese government changed the laws and wanted everyone to practice the same religion and have the same language. There was a protest and they started killing people, so my family had to run away to Nepal. When they got to Nepal, the Nepalese government didn't accept them and they had to be refugees. I was born in the refugee camp about nine years after my mom arrived there.

Life in the camp was hard. It wasn't very easy for me to live there because it was easy to see the native Nepali people didn't want us there. They would say things like, "You are not like us. You are from Bhutan, so go back to your country." I felt so bad about it. One day we heard about immigration. The government was trying to resettle the refugees and close the camps. We decided to move to the US.

At first, we had a problem with the processing of our visas. We had a cousin that was staying with us and since he wasn't eighteen, we had to contact his mother in India so that he could come with us. We also had to wait three years for him to turn eighteen so that he could come with us. When I heard that we were going to the US, I felt so happy, but at the same time I was also sad because I had to leave my friends. I was fourteen years old. When I went to the bus, I cried. It was really tough for me to leave my country, but I

43

was excited to move somewhere new.

I had never been on an airplane before, but I got used to it pretty quickly. To get to the US, we had to travel from Katmandu to Hong Kong, then to Los Angeles. When I got to Los Angeles, I was very thirsty and looked for water, but I couldn't find it. I asked one person where the water was. He showed me it was right in front of me. I felt so embarrassed because I had never seen a water fountain before. We just had a well for water.

When I got to Fargo, it was really cold outside. I had never seen snow before. It was the middle of winter—January 31, to be exact.

My aunts and my brothers came to pick us up, and a case manager came with them. When I saw my cousins, I saw that they had become taller than me. One of my cousins came over and I didn't recognize her.

Fargo was totally different from the camp. In the camp we lived in a small hut. When we first got here, we lived in an apartment. The apartments were huge, and they all looked the same. One time, I went into the wrong apartment by accident. Now we live in a house. The houses here in Fargo are much bigger than the camp huts.

I actually started school in seventh grade on Valentine's Day. My first day of school was kind of hard for me. I didn't know how to say things like, "May I go to the bathroom?" or "May I go get a drink?" I couldn't understand what most people were trying to say. Back in our country, we had English classes, but the teachers didn't speak very fast. Here, the teachers talked way faster than what I was used to, and I became confused. I made some Nepali friends there, so that was good.

When I was little, I started to dance. I normally danced by myself, but one day I performed at the school. I really didn't know how to dance well, but my teacher encouraged me to perform in front of others. That's how my dancing career got started.

Last summer I went to Akron, Ohio, for a Nepali dance competition. I got to meet lots of different people from different cities. I made lots of friends there, and it was one of the best chapters of my life.

I plan on going to college to get a medical doctorate degree so I can be a doctor and help different communities. In the refugee camp, we didn't have a great education. They did have a school there, but they really didn't teach us well enough. I want to become a doctor so that I can go back and help those in need.

greencardvoices.org/speakers/badal-mongar

Rutshuru, Democratic
Republic of the Congo

Divine Lubungo

From: Rutshuru, Democratic Republic of the Congo
Current City: Fargo, ND

> "GUNS WERE OUR MUSIC. MY SISTER AND I USED TO MAKE IT FUNNY. INSTEAD OF BEING SCARED LIKE MOST PEOPLE, WE WOULD MAKE FUN OF THE GUNS' SOUNDS AND PRETEND LIKE THEY WERE DRUMS."

I was born in Rutshuru, Congo. It is a small village. Life was pretty normal in my country. I was eight when I left. I lived with my mom because my father died when I was young. I actually grew up with a lot of family. I have nine big sisters, two big brothers, and I am the last-born.

Life was pretty good for me because I didn't really have to do a lot of chores. School wasn't really exciting because school in my country is a lot different. Teachers are really mean, and you would get beat up if you came late. To you guys it may seem strange, but if you were born and live in that country, it was completely normal.

Fear was normal in my country as well, because there was always a civil war. Most of the time I couldn't even understand why were they fighting. War broke out every day. Guns were our music. Instead of being scared like most people, my sister and I would make fun of the guns' sounds and pretend they were drums. It was scary, but eventually I got used to it.

I also remember some of the good things. I used to be kind of a wild kid. I loved to climb trees, although there were kind of dangerous trees. If I saw a mango, then I would go after it no matter how tall the tree was. My sister warned me multiple times, but I would never listen. I also loved to swim, but the river was far from my house. I used to try to help my mom with farming, but I wasn't good at it. But I tried to keep my mother company.

Like I said, I grew up without my dad, so my mom was like both parents, and raising eleven kids wasn't easy. Some of my sisters that were much older than me got married, and one of my sisters' husbands had a pretty decent job. She decided to take me and my other two sisters under her care. So I went to live with my sister. She also had kids: two boys, really stubborn, but cute.

It was just another normal day. My mom woke up in the morning and went out to the farm, but in the afternoon of that day, we started hearing rumors that there were some rebels breaking into nearby houses, killing people and raping women. We really didn't know what to do. My mom was not back. We thought it was not safe to stay in there because we had no idea when they were going to reach our house.

So my big sisters decided to take some money that my mom had saved and take us to Kampala, Uganda, because we heard that one of my sisters was living there now. Where we lived was a day-and-a-half walk to Uganda. So we decided to walk and save our money. When we reached Uganda, we crossed the border, took the bus, and joined our sister.

I lived in Uganda for about six years. Life was not really easy. It was a new country, so we had to speak a new language. They spoke Kiganda and English, and my country spoke Swahili and French. I had to learn two completely new languages. I tried to learn English at an English program school. They taught me for around three to six months. That's the only thing I did. I didn't go to school in Uganda.

Not everybody was welcoming in Uganda. Some people felt like we were invading their country. They used to tell us, "Go back to your country," or, "What are you doing in our country?" Although they understood that our country was not safe, I felt like they had a defensive mode in them, as if they felt like we were coming and taking over their country. Most of them would insult us, but some of them were friendly and welcoming.

Kampala is a really big city. I got lost easily, and most of the stuff was pretty expensive. Finding a job also is really difficult, and my sister struggled with that. I had to sit at home because there was really no money for me to go to school. Life in Uganda was not easy; it was difficult, but we survived.

Since we were refugees in Uganda, we joined some refugee programs. There were a couple different refugee programs in Uganda. They helped people from war-affected countries get to a safer place. Some of the programs send refugees to the US and some send them to Europe. That's how we got into the US. It was a really long process and took a long time and lots of patience.

I remember that day. I was so, so happy. We were at the dinner table when my sister said that she had something to tell us. Everybody was anxious. We actually thought that it was either us or her boys that were in trouble so we all started just ask our questions at once. She then told us that it was actually good news, but she wanted us to finish eating because she didn't want us to get too excited and lose our appetite. We didn't even have the appetite to eat, so we kept asking the questions. That's when she told us that we had our visas and we were going to the US in two weeks.

For me, it was the best news ever because the US was my dream country. I was so happy and excited. We had to go through some processing as well as orientation. They also had to educate us about life in the US.

I remember stepping into the airport. It was my first time, and the building was so big and smelled so fresh. We had to wait around six or seven hours for the plane to come. With all of our excitement, it felt like torture, but it was worth it. The flight attendants directed us to our seats on this big airplane, and I sat right next to my brother. They didn't let me bring the food that I had, since that was against the rules, so I just fell asleep hungry. I don't know how many hours I slept.

My brother woke me up when the airplane food arrived, and to be honest, I really enjoyed the food—except for the cheese. In Uganda, cheese was very expensive, so it was more of a delicacy. I wasn't used to the taste, so I didn't find the cheese that great. The sound inside the plane bothered me a lot. I'm not sure how many planes we took, but we went from Uganda to Belgium, Belgium to Chicago, and Chicago to Fargo.

When we landed in Fargo, there were two ladies waiting for us. They introduced themselves as case managers from Lutheran Social Services and told us they were going to be the ones to help us adapt to Fargo. Fargo wasn't the big city that I imagined, but the autumn weather was really pretty.

I was really surprised by the overall structure of the city. The roads were well maintained, there were sidewalks everywhere, and the grass just seemed natural. Seeing the highway was really amazing because it was my first time seeing one. As we drove, I stuck my head out the window for a quick second to enjoy the experience.

Our first apartment was near a park, which made me happy since I had a place to go and play. I was also scared, however, because I didn't really speak English that much. Ugandan English is much different than American English, and since I didn't go to school, I didn't speak that much English. I did have some basic knowledge though.

I started school in October. The school system was totally different here. The way teachers taught, the loose dress code, everything. Because I didn't speak that much English, I went from the cheerful kid who talked too much to the quiet kid who watched everyone. It was really difficult for me to adapt because I'm not really good at making friends.

One positive thing about school was my teachers. They were absolutely amazing. My EL teachers were really helpful in every class that I had. They also helped me make new friends. School here wasn't nearly as strict as it was back in Congo, which was nice. I also enjoyed the many different activities that I could get involved in, such as sports, debate, student congress, and choir.

In this three years, I have learned a lot and improved a lot. I'm still picking up new things every single day. I have a job now. I've been working at Noodles & Company a year now, and that's not the only place I've worked. I've also worked at Culver's. I worked there for seven months.

I played basketball all my freshman year, but unfortunately, I came down with asthma, so I can't play any sports. I love to sing, so I was also in choir. Since this year is senior year, I have taken the required classes that will allow me to graduate and go to college. I'm starting to think a lot about my future now and trying my best to prepare for what is ahead.

Ever since I was a little kid, I wanted to work in a hospital. I love helping others. When I started to look into college last year though, I found out that being a doctor is really expensive and it also takes a long time. As a result, I want to become a dental hygienist now. I still hope to work in a hospital, but this will require less money and less school. Who knows, though. It might change. I just want to be happier, live my life the way I want to live it, and hopefully get married.

VIDEO LINKS

greencardvoices.org/speakers/divine-lubungo

Lagos,Nigeria

Quazeem Adeyinka

From: Lagos, Nigeria
Current City: Fargo, ND

"THE HAPPIEST MOMENT OF MY LIFE WAS WHEN I TOUCHED DOWN IN AMERICA TO BE REUNITED WITH MY MOTHER AND SISTER."

I was born in western Lagos, Nigeria. Life in Africa was rough, but it was also fun. I had my family and my friends. When I came to America, the only sad thing about leaving Lagos was that I left tons of family and friends back there. I talk to them everyday now, and I miss them very much.

I have six siblings. When I was born I lived with my parents. My childhood was very fun. I grew up with older people, so I was pampered. My parents were old so everything was obviously in my favor because I was the youngest. When I was growing up, all my brothers were getting married and moving out. I mostly stayed indoors and always got what I wanted. My father died in 2009.

In my elementary school, all my teachers liked me because I was very smart. My father was the chairman of the school, which made me the most popular kid. Secondary school, unfortunately, got very tough. I was unable to get a scholarship no matter how hard I tried. When I was supposed to graduate, however, I got my visa to come to America.

I've been in America since January 15, 2016. I arrived at the airport in Baltimore, Maryland. The happiest moment of my life was when I touched down in America to be reunited with my mother and sister. My mother left for the United States to live with my older sister who is in Maryland. My older sister and I get along well, so she wanted me to come live with her. I applied for a student visa. I lived with my sister and mom there.

One of my uncles lives in Fargo. We used talk on the phone for two or three hours almost every day. He is a bachelor and lives alone, so he lied to me and told me that Fargo was fun and that I should come and join him. So I decided to come here. I spent three days traveling to Fargo on the bus. When I finally got to Fargo, I realized that everything he told me were just lies. I was so, so angry, but I had no choice but to stay.

Now, I am a sophomore. I came very late in the 2015–16 school year, so I wasn't an official student, but I attended classes because I wanted to. School here is very, very different than school in Africa. In Africa, you are always afraid of the teachers because they are superior and they have a certain set of rules that you cannot break. If you break them, then they whip you or beat you. Schools here allow us to use gadgets in class where as in Africa there are only certain times when gadgets are permitted for educational usage. I'm getting used to the American ways, and it has been pretty difficult.

The EL English teacher, Mrs. Juelke, is like a mother to me. She is more like a counselor even though she is just my teacher. She is one of the few teachers that I really like because, when I was new here, she welcomed me and made me feel accepted. She is also one of the few teachers who understands my accent and myself overall.

"You can take me out of Nigeria, but you cannot take Nigeria out of me." I still live the Nigerian life. I'm not used to the American culture and I'm really, really having problems with that. For example, my accent. I have a deep African accent and I don't think people understand what I am saying. That's very excruciating for me. The only people that understand me are Mrs. Juelke and a few of my friends.

My life has been difficult in America so far. There was a time when I was here I didn't want to go out of the door, even to go to the store. I didn't like going alone because when I tried to communicate I would say the same thing three or four times before people understood me. I think things are getting better now.

I'm still young, and I don't really have it all planned out. There's a saying that goes, "Hope for the best and prepare for the worst." Right now I really can't tell because I haven't made a decision. I'm an athlete. I'm a good soccer player. I'm hoping to go to college to study law.

greencardvoices.org/speakers/quazeem-adeyinka

Lusaka, Zambia

Aziza Kabura

From: Lusaka, Zambia
Current City: Fargo, ND

"MY MOM EXPLAINED THAT THERE ARE MANY DIFFERENT KINDS OF PEOPLE IN AMERICA AND WE SHOULD BE RESPECTFUL TO ALL OF THEM."

My name is Aziza Kabura and I was born in Lusaka, Zambia. My mom was originally from Burundi, but because of the war, she moved to Zambia. My father is from Congo and also went to Zambia. They married in 1999, and I was born in 2001.

When I was around six years old, my family moved to the Maheba refugee camp because my dad wasn't happy with how others were treating us like foreigners because we weren't Zambian. We moved to the refugee camp because anyone, despite his or her nationality, can live freely in the camp. Thus, we ended up staying at the camp for three years.

The camp was fairly large, and we technically lived in a smaller sub-division called Maheba D. Despite this, it was still pretty crowded. The area was filled with trees, animals, and people. Some people were attempting to cultivate food for themselves to eat. My house was actually quite big because my father worked hard for us to be comfortable. Despite this, life was still somewhat difficult. It was hard for me to understand other people because I did not know how to speak their languages, such as Swahili and Kirundi. Luckily, because I grew up speaking English, schoolwork was easy for me, since they used English as the primary language in the camp's school.

After living in the camp, we were allowed to move to anywhere because we had a special card. We moved back to Lusaka, Zambia, and lived there for a total of four years. During those four years my brother was born. We then moved to Solwezi, Zambia.

It took my parents sixteen years to get us a spot to go to America. Some people we knew were going to Canada and the UK. Immigration told us the day that we were going and that we would go to Lusaka and then to the airport. We stayed in a hotel for a week so we could do our medical checks.

57

At first, being on an airplane was scary because I had never been in an airplane before. I started crying. I thought I would die. It took us two hours to reach South Africa. We had to remove our shoes and any metals that we had on us, like belts, earrings, and watches. They checked if there were any bad things in there.

After that we went to a huge airplane. It was amazing, but I didn't like the food. I had not slept since we started the journey twenty-two hours before. I was like, "I'm not sleeping. I will die." I was really scared. I was sitting beside my dad and my mom was sitting with my brother. We went from South Africa to New York, then to Dallas, Texas.

Seeing our new apartment in America was kind of weird at first. I thought, "Why am I in this place?" I thought there would be more people outside playing, talking to each other. The social worker told us that if you were going to somebody's place you had to notify them that you were coming. In Africa, it is okay just to show up at someone's place unannounced.

I saw a lot of people speaking Spanish; I wondered who these people were. Why were they so short and I so tall? Why didn't they like me? They were white, I was black. My mom explained that there are many kinds of people in America, and we should be respectful to all of them.

In Africa I was in ninth grade. In America, they were telling me that I had to start in eighth grade. I was fourteen, so they said I was too young for high school.

They took me to a middle school where I had to wear a uniform. Certain grades wore certain colors. I didn't like wearing the uniforms at all. I told my teachers that I didn't want to go to school. They told me that if I missed school, my parents would get in trouble. So I went. The way the teachers taught was confusing, and I didn't like moving from class to class. In Africa, the teacher moves from class to class and the students stay in the same room. My dad had a hard time finding a job, so we had to move. My dad didn't speak English, and they only wanted to hire English speakers. I wanted to stay there in Houston with my uncle, but my parents did not let me. At first I was upset. It was the same feeling I had when I came from Africa to Texas.

We moved to Fargo. After two weeks, I went to take a test to get into school. I started at the middle school. They put me in upper level classes. I made some friends and started to get used to life in Fargo.

I went to summer school and I met a lot of people. I made friends and it was fun. After summer school, I started high school. I realized I had to be serious. I started watching videos about high school on YouTube.

When I started at Fargo South High, I was amazed by how huge it was. I thought I would get lost. Luckily, I found my friends from summer school and they helped me find my classes.

My favorite subjects are math, English, and science. After school, I play soccer with my friends. My dream is to study hard and go to college. I would like to study science and do something with medicine. After I have accomplished my first dream, I wish to go back to Africa, build a house and a school. It would be a free school, because most schools in Africa cost money and many people can't pay for school. I want to help kids learn, have a better future, and be happy.

greencardvoices.org/speakers/aziza-kabura

Baghdad, Iraq

Ashti Mohamed Ali

From: Baghdad, Iraq
Current City: Fargo, ND

"A HUGE MISCONCEPTION OF IRAQ IS THAT IT IS VERY POOR. IT'S ACTUALLY A REALLY RICH COUNTRY AND WE HAVE A LOT OF MALLS, STORES, ROADS, RESTAURANTS, ETC. SO TO ME, FARGO WASN'T THAT DIFFERENT AT ALL."

My name is Ashti Mohamed Ali, and I was born in Baghdad, Iraq. I have four siblings: one older brother, one twin brother, and two sisters. Life in Iraq, as I recall, was actually pretty good. It was always hot, and I remember spending a lot of my time with my family, hanging out with my friends, and going to school. As Baghdad became more dangerous, however, my family and I started going out less and less. It was just too risky and dangerous, and unfortunately our whole family became threatened as well.

My father was an interpreter with the US Army, which was a very dangerous job. In fact, the Iraqi army told him that if he didn't move to another country, then there would be a high chance that he would be killed. As a result, we had no choice but to first move out of Baghdad into the northern countryside and then sign up for the immigration program.

To be completely honest though, my family initially didn't want to leave. I remember that one night when I was sleeping, my sister woke me up. I couldn't fall back asleep, so I went to see my mother. She was mad, which surprised me. When I asked her why she was mad, she told us that my dad wanted us to go to the United States, so he applied our whole family for the immigration program. My mother was angry because she didn't want to leave behind our family, our neighbors, our land, and our country. I, on the other hand, was more happy, and after convincing my mother that the US would be much safer, she finally caved in and we were all on board.

The application process took about four and a half years, but in the end, we were accepted. I remember the night before we left we went to visit our relatives. We had kept this whole thing a secret up until that point, and when we told them, they were in complete shock. We all cried together, had dinner, and gave good-bye hugs and kisses.

As for the trip, we flew from Iraq to Jordan, then from Jordan to Chicago, and finally from Chicago to Fargo. We stayed over in Jordan for one day, and the rest of the trip was continuous. It was my first time on the airplane, and I was so terrified. I didn't like the food they served and didn't really eat much, but despite this I was happy because I was finally moving to the US.

When we first got to the airport, I saw my cousins and I cried out in happiness because I hadn't seen them for about six years. We greeted and hugged each other, and after that, my cousin's girlfriend, who is actually American, gave us a ride to our apartment. It was only my sister and me in her car, and she was speaking English to us, but we didn't understand a single word she said. That was kind of awkward moment. It was April then, and I remember how cold I felt because I was only used to the warm weather we had back at home.

Thankfully, our cousin had already rented an apartment for us, so we had a place to settle down right away. While I thought I was going to be shocked by the change in landscape, I wasn't. Honestly, I didn't think that the roads and stores were that different than they were back in Iraq. A huge misconception of Iraq is that it is very poor. It's actually a really rich country, and we have a lot of malls, stores, roads, restaurants, etc. So to me, Fargo wasn't that different at all. What I was surprised by, however, was the diversity of people here. For example, I had never seen a black person before, so when I first saw one, I was actually quite shocked. The mixture of culture and diversity was what I found to be truly unique.

As for school, I am a senior in high school. Back in Iraq, I was a senior, but because of my lack of English, they placed me in as a sophomore here. However, it has been two and a half years, so now I am officially a senior again.

My favorite subject is science. I love science. Science is seen everywhere and it plays a huge role in almost everything we do in life. Initially, I hated English because it was so difficult for me. But luckily, my cousin's girlfriend is an American, so we spoke with her almost everyday and she taught us basic phrases and helped us learn English at home. Now English is one of my favorite subjects as well.

Aside from school, I also started working at JCPenney in 2014 and also play tennis here at Fargo South High. In the future, I plan on studying to become an orthopedic surgeon as well as fulfilling my dream of traveling the world. I guess that's pretty much it.

greencardvoices.org/speakers/ashti-mohamed-ali

...ills and its application. Use 3-D modeling software to design ...ms and communicate solutions to peers.

Engineering: Grades 10-12

...lving skills and apply knowledge... ...Topics include mechanisms...

...ring and Architec...

...s aspects of civil engine...

...al design software to...

...w it all fits t...

...inate solutions to ...matics.

...l and commercial struct...

Engineeri

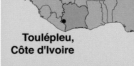

Toulépleu,
Côte d'Ivoire

Pleasure Jerue

From: Toulépleu, Côte d'Ivoire
Current City: Fargo, ND

> "IT'S ACTUALLY HELPFUL NOW THAT I KNOW IT'S OKAY TO BE WHO YOU ARE, TO SPEAK A DIFFERENT LANGUAGE, TO COME FROM SOMEWHERE ELSE, AND YOU DON'T HAVE TO BE EMBARRASSED ABOUT IT, WHICH MAKES ME REALLY HAPPY."

I was born in the Toulépleu region in the village of Duble, Côte d'Ivoire. My father was Liberian and my mother was Ivorian. My older sister and I were in Côte d'Ivoire for a while, and my mom would always like to dress us up in the same clothes. It was really funny. Then the war happened and we had to move to Liberia, where my father was staying. My older brother went to my step-mother, I believe, and that's when we stayed in the refugee camps for a while.

The refugee camps weren't really fun. We had a small tent. There were rations, and my mother said that she pretty much gave us most of the food because she thought we were her biggest priority. She didn't really eat as much, and my father was about to go fight in the war. My father stayed because my mother begged him to. I thank him today that we are actually here in America.

My father thought about registering us to come to America. By then my older sister and I went with my father. He applied and it took a while before we could even come here. When we were able to, my mother had to stay behind because my father hadn't filled in everything yet. My father told me that he had to sign them quickly or we would've been in Africa to this day. We wouldn't have been able to come to America. Unfortunately though, my older brother, Augustin, is still in Africa. We're trying to apply for him to come to America now, but complications remain. I believe it was a year before my mother could come to America, and I didn't stay with my father. My mother and my father and my older sister were all together, but I lived with my auntie who was in Minnesota. I stayed with her until I was four or five, so I wasn't really with my father or my family when we came to America. I was with someone else who I thought was like a mother figure, 'cause my mother wasn't around.

Even though I was one year old when we came to America, I somehow knew that I was in a new place. Things weren't right, and America was just way too new for me. It took a lot for me, since I wasn't really with my family, and when my father came to get me I thought he was a stranger. I referred to my auntie as "Ma" since she was the figure in my life when my mother wasn't there. So far I've been with my family now, but it's still a little bit awkward when my auntie comes around and my mom is there because I still refer to my auntie as "Ma."

I was in Minneapolis, Minnesota, and then we moved around a lot. We went to Grand Forks, and from Grand Forks we moved to Sioux Falls, and then we came down here to Fargo. That's when I registered at Woodrow Wilson. Starting out, I didn't really know English that well. In fact, I'm still struggling with English, even if it may be hard to tell. My mother went there too to learn English, and learning English was pretty hard. My father, however, was kind of the "light" in moving to America. He practiced English, and he got it, and it was pretty much him who registered us into everything.

I went to Woodrow Wilson for one year. After that I went to Jefferson, and I was in an EL class for another year before I was actually able to join the other kids and be able to associate with them. I sort of felt like an outcast since I had to go to EL. It was always, "Speak English", "Do English", "Do you know English?" And I struggled with it. I did my best even though it kind of made me feel bad about myself that I didn't know the language that everyone spoke. But in America, especially in Fargo, most people like to help.

My parents started moving from Grand Forks, to Sioux Falls, and finally to Fargo because it's where my relatives were. Since we were new to Fargo, and America in general, we didn't know exactly where to go, and since they were here first, we thought it would be best to stay with them. In Sioux Falls I stayed with another auntie, and living there was when I first experienced winter. From Sioux Falls we came to Fargo, and we haven't moved yet.

I didn't know what snow was, where it came from, or what it does. In fact, I believe that it was in Sioux Falls that I got my first frostbite on my right ear. It was super uncomfortable.

Since we moved from Sioux Falls to Fargo, I think the person I've looked up to most is my older sister because she has told me to keep my head high and to always go through school. And my parents because they always say, "Read books, do your homework, and when you're done, have fun." They believe education comes first, and after that you can have fun with your life.

I really thank my mother and my father for making us get this far in life and never giving up on us.

My older sister, who is going to school with me now, is really amazing. I see just how far she's gone, and just how good in school she is, because she really puts school first. No matter what obstacles come in her way, such as English, she always says: "You're gonna be fine, just go through it." I feel super happy every time that I speak English now because I feel like I'm American. I can talk to people and I can associate with them. From reading books I've become really, really happy, and I've gone far.

I've made sure to always read and try to get into mechanical engineering. For someone who came from outside, it's very different, but I enjoy learning it everyday. I tell my father, and he just supports me along the way and never judges me. None of my family members do, which always makes me happy. When I say that to my teachers, I feel even happier because they tell me to strive for excellence.

The language that we speak at home is like an African-English, where we have different accents. We also speak Krahn and French. I believe that Krahn is what my father teaches me everyday, and French is from my mom. Learning both those languages also helps here because most African people here speak French. If you speak French, you can associate with them as well. I also like speaking my African-English because I like to confuse people.

It's through speaking that they ask me "Oh, where are you from?" or "Where did you get this accent from?" I feel happy now. Now that I know that it's actually okay to be different, instead of American and only speaking English. It's actually helpful now that I know it's okay to be who you are, to speak a different language, to come from somewhere else, and you don't have to be embarrassed about it, which makes me really happy.

I want to be a mechanical engineer because I've realized that technology really runs the world now. I've always been fascinated by how it helps everyone. I've read books about putting things together and taking them apart and seeing how they function and work. I just want to expand in that region because I can help so many people. It's really made me think about people in general, and how technology really helps us and brings us together without us really knowing it. I've also taken a fascination in it because of my father, who does a lot of engineering and just looks so amazing when he does it. That kind of makes me want to do the same thing. I just want to strive for excellence like my father and hopefully bring technology to other people who really need it.

Since coming to America, I've realized that the food is absolutely different. I find that there are a lot of restaurants; hamburgers and fries are the two main things, and then there's pizza. I haven't really liked pizza; it just doesn't fascinate me. When I go back home, I realize my culture is rice, fufu, and water.

I realize that there's so many cultures here as well, such as Mexican and Chinese, and you have to get used to this or that. You go to a restaurant that has another culture and you're like, "Oh my God, I can't believe this is all in America." I'm glad I came here, because now I can see just how far America spans out. There are so many cultures in this place that I am just so fascinated by. I'm glad that my father and my whole entire family strived to actually bring us here, and that I'm here and I can help other people who are new here. I'm just glad to say that I'm American.

---

greencardvoices.org/speakers/pleasure-jerue

Cairo, Egypt

Mesaged Abakar

From: Cairo, Egypt
Current City: Fargo, ND

> "I WAS EXCITED TO COME HERE BUT I WAS ALSO SAD BECAUSE I HAD BEEN WITH MY FRIENDS FOR A LONG TIME AND IT'S SAD TO JUST LEAVE AND NOT KNOW IF YOU'RE GOING TO COME BACK OR NOT."

My parents are from Sudan, but they moved to Egypt, and that's where I was born. When I was in Egypt, I had two brothers: Muhend and Yousef. We had school off on Friday because that's when we had to go pray. We had Saturdays off as well. We had school on Sunday. My best friend was on the basketball team. One time her dad brought me to practice with her and I played a little bit and really enjoyed it. That's when I started liking basketball. After I realized basketball was really fun, I would go down by my apartment and just dribble or play with people.

We lived in Cairo. School started pretty early, so we'd wake up at five or six in the morning. When we got to school, we had a ritual where we would say an anthem, a couple of students would read part of the Quran, and we would repeat after them. There was a tutoring class either before or after school that parents would pay for for their kids to get help and stay ahead in school.

At our school, our classes were like elementary school, where you just have one class and two different teachers. For each grade, there were about two to three different classes. We didn't have a bell and passing times like we do here. School would be over around two o'clock, and I'd go home around five or six o'clock and do my homework and sometimes go outside with some of my friends because the weather was always good.

When I found out we were coming to America, we knew what city we were gonna be in, so I looked it up on the computer and it looked pretty cool. I was excited to come here but I was also sad because I had been with my friends for a long time, and it's sad to just leave and not know if you're going to come back or not. For a while, my friends didn't know the truth, so they just thought that I was going on a vacation somewhere for a while and even-

71

tually coming back. When they found out, they were pretty sad too. When we came here, it was my first time on a plane, so it was kind of scary because I'm afraid of heights.

Egypt was different from Fargo. In Egypt, apartments are usually around six stories high or higher. When we came here, our apartment was only about three stories. In Egypt, we would have only four apartments next to each other, but here there are about six or seven on a floor. Here, if you walk in the buildings, people under you would hear you, but in Egypt, even if you run, people underneath you would not hear you. Police officers here roam around and watch you. In Egypt, you wouldn't see a police car driving by your apartment.

We came in the summer of 2012, so I just went straight to summer school for a couple of days. When I walked into the class, it was really different because in Egypt there were chalkboards and four people sat together at the same desk. Here there are separate desks for each student. At first, it was hard learning English. I thought school was going be really hard and that I wouldn't understand most of the things, but it turned out to be easier than I had expected. People were really friendly. I thought it was really weird that we had school in the summer because, in Egypt, we don't have summer school.

I started basketball in fifth grade, and I really liked it and thought it was something I wanted to do in the future. I am still playing basketball right now and plan on joining the basketball team. Playing in fifth grade was a little hard, but it got easier as time went on. I thought it was weird that they had sports after school because in Egypt, they don't.

There are a lot of teachers here compared to how many we had back in Egypt. Freshman year is actually very easy. From what a lot of people had said about high school, it sounded difficult, but once I got used to it, it turned out to be a lot different from what I had expected. In Egypt, my favorite subject was science, but here it was a lot different than what I learned. Science seemed harder. So my favorite subject is actually English. I just think it's really easy.

I think it's a lot easier to make friends now, especially because I am in sports. When I go to meets and games, I just meet a lot of people. Most people are friendly, but there are some people who just don't like you for no reason. They're just rude.

I wanted to be a basketball coach, but now I want to become a lawyer.

I'm working on that now by getting good grades. I just joined student congress and debate, and I want to be involved in everything that has to do with law. I also want to go to college because it's better for the future. If you don't go to college, you might end up working at, say, a McDonalds. That's not bad, but you won't earn as much money. If you went to college and graduate, you would have a degree and you would get a better job. It just makes life easier and you learn a lot more.

I was thinking of working, but I just want to focus on school. Especially because basketball is starting soon so I won't really have much time to go to basketball, work, do all my homework, and focus if I get a job. If I do work, it's just going be in the summer.

---

greencardvoices.org/speakers/mesaged-abakar

Jhapa, Nepal

Roshika Nepal

From: Jhapa, Nepal
Current City: Fargo, ND

"I REMEMBER THAT I CRIED WHEN I HAD TO LEAVE THE REFUGEE CAMP BECAUSE I WAS LEAVING EVERYTHING BEHIND."

Our life was pretty poor. We used to live in a mud house, and there were a lot of people there. I was born in Timai camp. My mom used to wake us up early. Our life was pretty fun there even though we lived in a poor city. I lived there for eight years, and I was in third grade when I came here.

I have six members in my family: two brothers, one sister, mom, and dad. My hobbies were playing with friends and hanging out with them. My mom and dad used to live in a farm that was one hour away from the Timai camp, so I used to go there every Friday and stay for two days. When I got back to the camp, I would go to school.

Our school was made out of bamboo and cement. We used to sit on the carpet and our teacher hit us when we didn't get our homework done. My parents came from Bhutan, and I was born ten years later. My parents lived in a refugee camp for a total of eighteen years.

I remember the day we heard that we were going to America. My dad was sitting on a bench and my sister just came and said, "Mom, Mom, our date is near, the date to come to America," and she was so shocked. My neighbor was there with my dad, and I was really excited. I was thinking about how it would be hard to learn the language, but we would have a better education. I said to my mom, "I can't wait to go to America."

I remember that I cried when I had to leave the refugee camp because I was leaving everything behind. I was leaving my friends behind forever and some family members too. I had lived there for eight years. It was kind of a sad moment.

The International Organization for Migration drove us on a bus to Chandragadhi Airport. From there our journey began. We drove to Kathmandu, where we stayed for seven days, and then we flew to Hong Kong. We stayed there for three hours and then flew to New York. From there, we went to Chicago and then, finally, to Fargo. Our journey was kind of difficult and kind of fun. We didn't know anything. We stayed in a hotel in New York, and they gave us food. We ate peas, and we didn't like them because we were used to spicy food and rice. It was totally different food. At the airport, everybody was white, so it was kind of different from back home.

We came to Fargo on December 1, 2010. It was snowing. It was really cold outside, and my uncle picked us up from the airport. We lived in his house for like five days before we moved to our house. Our house was pretty clean. Everything was organized, and we were pretty excited.

It was different because the apartment had a table and chairs. Back home, we used to sit on the floor and eat. The new kitchen also had a stove. Back home, we used the fire to cook our food. It took a couple days to learn how to use these items. We used to have bamboo beds, and here we have a mattress. There were a lot of cupboards in the kitchen. We used to make cabinets out of bamboos to put our cups and plates in. And back home we didn't have a rice cooker.

The first days were pretty hard. Everything was white outside, and we didn't go out a lot because it was December and really cold. We visited some new people that came from a different refugee camp.

Starting school in Fargo was like a whole new world. I felt like I was the only Nepalese person in the whole school. I was in third grade at the time, and there were a few Nepali students, but they were in first grade and kindergarten. So, it was kind of difficult. I didn't understand what people were saying because they spoke so fast. I'm getting used to America now. I'm feeling more comfortable here. Now I can understand what the teachers are saying. My English is getting better each and every day.

My hope is to go back to my country one day and visit everyone there. I also have a dream to become an actress one day.

greencardvoices.org/speakers/roshika-nepal

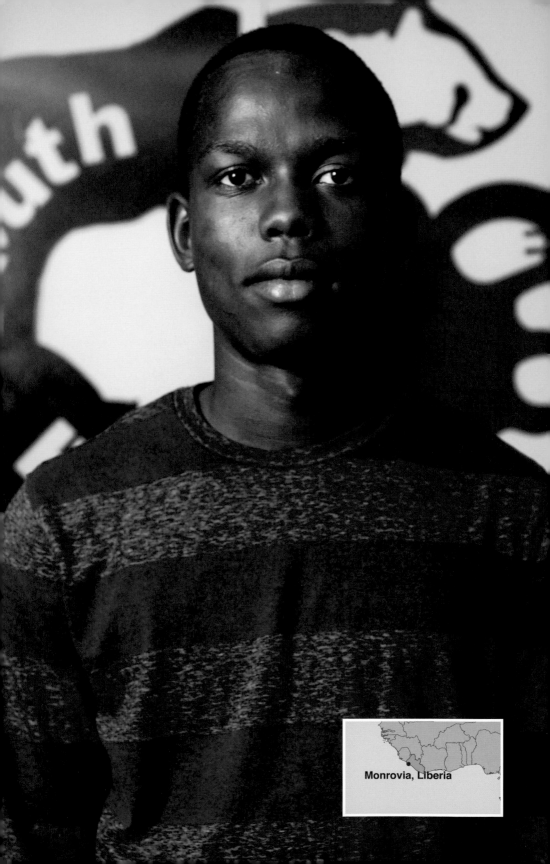

Monrovia, Liberia

Alvin Johnson

From: Monrovia, Liberia
Current City: Fargo, ND

> "ON OUR WAY HOME FROM THE AIRPORT, MY MOM STOPPED AT THE STORE AND BOUGHT SPAGHETTI. THIS WAS THE FIRST FOOD I ATE IN AMERICA AND IT WAS SO GOOD."

I was born in Liberia. My life there was fine, but school there was so hard. When I was ten years old, my mom came to America and she spent six years here; she played DV (Diversity Visa Lottery). When I was sixteen, she sent for me and my sister to come to America. My mom worked with a local church to help bring us to the United States.

Back home in Africa, I went to a Catholic school. The school was very difficult and some of the students were not good. I miss a lot of friends back home. I always had a lot of fun playing soccer back home.

I remember the day that my mom and dad told me we were coming to America. One Sunday morning, April 15, my parents called, and my dad said me and my sister would leave later that month for America. I was so happy. Next, my dad sent money to buy our plane tickets and clothes for our travels. I was so excited at the thought of seeing my dad and mom.

The plane ride to America was my first time riding a plane; I was so scared. We landed in New York and got stuck at the airport, so my mom had to come pick us up there. On our way home from the airport, my mom stopped at the store and bought spaghetti. This was the first food I ate in America and it was so good.

Back in April, on the first day we were here, I got to see my mom's house. I was happy that she had her own house. It was my dad's house, too, but he worked in New Jersey doing construction, so he was not always home. The first day we were here, my mom bought us new clothes and new shoes. On the second day, we already had to start school. In school, I met a lot of friends; people seemed to like me. I joined the school soccer team.

School here is okay; I like it better than at home. Back at home, school was much harder and teachers could beat the students. I feel safer here because teachers cannot beat students. My favorite subjects are science, social studies, and computers. In the future, I want to work in construction, like my dad. I want to be just like my dad.

I like that my family is all together here in America; it's good to be together. Me, my sister, my dad, and my mom have fun together.

---

greencardvoices.org/speakers/alvin-johnson

Uvira, Democratic
Republic of the Congo

Esperance Mfurakazi

From: Uvira, Democratic Republic of the Congo
Current City: Fargo, ND

> "IN KENYA, WE HAD HOUSES MADE OUT OF STONES BUT OUR HOUSE HERE LOOKED LIKE IT MIGHT GET BLOWN OVER EASILY BY THE WIND."

My name is Esperance Mfurakazi. I was born in Uvira, Congo. My family and I lived a happy life, but then the war started and that changed everything. We then ended up moving to Burundi.

Life was different in Burundi because we didn't know the language. We were in a refugee camp so everyone had to stay in the camp itself. It was hard getting used to it at first because it was my first time in a refugee camp.

When we arrived, the camp was peaceful. However, a few days later at around eight p.m., my family and I were sleeping when we heard some people shouting for help. My dad was with my uncle in a separate part of the camp. We were scared, so my mom decided to take a look outside. She told us to hide. She went outside with another woman and immediately the woman got shot and died. We were scared and confused because we didn't know what was going on.

After a while, we heard people shouting, and we thought that they were coming to help, but actually, those were the people who were trying to kill us. They were calling to the people in the camp to come out so that they could shoot them. So many people were burned alive that day, including my father, who one of killers took and burned after he saw us going towards him.

We were all scared and at a complete loss of words. The men who killed my father thought that my mother was dead as well. After debating with one of his friends, one of the killers decided to let us live, since they thought that we couldn't get far in life because both of our parents were dead. We felt like we didn't have anywhere to go either because more than half the people we knew in that camp were killed as well.

My older sister told us to run away from the camp and meet up with other people who were trying to escape from the camp. When we were run-

83

ning away, we saw our aunt who fortunately was alive. We told her that our mother was dead, since that's what we heard from our father's killers, and our aunt brought us over to her camp house.

When we were at my aunt's place, the people once again called for those inside the camp to come out. One of my aunt's daughters went out and she was shot and killed as well. When these killers saw that no one was coming out, they set fire to the camp and burned those who were in their camp houses. Luckily, my aunt took us and we escaped from the camp. Later on, we found out that within two hours, 166 people had died.

The next day, those who survived were taken to a hospital. My aunt was being treated because she was shot in her side. When she was in the hospital, she asked us if we heard anything about our mother. We didn't say anything. Then, another person told us that our mother was looking for us. We were shocked because we thought that our mother was dead. When the person as well as hospital employees volunteered to show us where our mother was, we all thought that they were taking us to see her corpse so we said no and decided to stay with our aunt. Our aunt was angry because she couldn't believe they would do such a thing to us little kids. Thankfully, the woman kept insisting that our mother was alive and that she had seen her outside. Finally, my aunt told us to go and look outside for our uncle and cousins. We couldn't find them, and just when we were about to walk in, we saw my mother. My siblings and I couldn't believe our eyes. We cried because it was such a miracle that she was still alive.

We didn't want to leave Burundi at first because we didn't want to leave our father behind. He died in Burundi, and we couldn't just leave him. We didn't go back to the camp, so we settled in this place called Bujumbura, which was actually far from town. My mother found a job and we lived there for five years. Then in 2009, my mother decided that it was finally time for us to move on and that it was an opportunity for us to change our lives, so we moved to Nairobi, Kenya.

When we got to Nairobi, we didn't have any hope of coming to America, but it was a good chance to start a new life. There were UN employees who provided us with documents so that we could legally live there. We prayed to God quite often not only for saving us but perhaps for showing us a new path of peace and happiness. People just wanted peace. That was what was on everybody's mind. Peace and happiness.

In terms of life in Nairobi, I was lucky because somebody was willing to pay for my school. I went to school there and I was in form 3 (which is like junior year of high school). One day my mom came to visit me in school and told me that we were going to America. I was shocked and didn't believe it. As a stroke of luck, the UN approved us as refugees to go to the United States. I didn't believe it at all but it was the absolute truth. Within a month, we received our medication and other important forms of information for coming to the US. So after living in Nairobi for six years, we were coming to America.

Leaving Nairobi was sad for me because I was going to say good-bye to those that I had known for six years. I was also anxious because I was unsure of how I was going to get used to another life again. Everything in that moment was quite confusing.

Our journey was quite stressful due to the differences in languages and the fact that it was our first time going on a journey of this length. Because I went to school, I knew a bit of English, so I was an interpreter for us at the airport in Kenya and helped my mother navigate the airport and board our plane. I don't really recall much of the trip, only the fact that the food on the plane wasn't good. I remember craving Kenya's food instead of the airplane food.

When we got to Fargo, we saw my uncle waiting for us. It was surprising to us because we hadn't seen him in about ten years. We had only heard rumors of him being alive and living in America. We embraced each other and we all cried because finally, after so long, it finally felt like we had a family again.

It was March and the weather, to us anyways, was way too cold. We weren't used to it at all. It was so windy, and we were all thinking that Kenya was better than this country weatherwise. People were joking with us that if we went outside and touched the snow with our hands would fall off. We were surprised but happy at the same time.

When we got to Fargo, we liked the city but were afraid of our house because it looked too flimsily built. In Kenya, we had houses made out of stones, but our house here looked like it might get blown over easily by the wind. We soon found out that that wasn't true.

I initially had to go to the ninth grade. I tried to explain to them that I was in form 3, so I should enroll in eleventh grade, but they told me that I had to start from the very bottom. Luckily, my mother brought some of my academic records from Kenya, and after seeing that I had the experience needed, they decided to put me in tenth grade instead, which is where I started.

Now, I feel much more comfortable in this school system. My favorite subjects are math and science. Those have always been my favorite since I was a kid, because I knew that when I grew up I was going to be a doctor. I have always been driven to help people from my country who need help or are unable to pay for their medication. Being a doctor is still my dream today. My overall goal is to be able to save up enough money and help my family and friends back at home in Burundi or Kenya. I also hope to travel back to Africa as a doctor and be able to give them the care they deserve.

---

greencardvoices.org/speakers/esperance-mfurakazi

Lomé, Togo

Godwin Kouhe

From: Lomé, Togo
Current City: Fargo, ND

"I SAW COMPUTERS AND HUGE FLAT SCREEN TVS AND THAT IS ACTUALLY HOW I BECAME INTERESTED IN TECHNOLOGY. I BECAME CURIOUS BECAUSE I DIDN'T KNOW HOW SUCH BEAUTIFUL TECHNOLOGY WORKED."

I was born in the city of Lomé in Togo. I pretty much lived with my uncle and aunt for most of my life, which was actually pretty good. I mostly had fun with my family. I got along with my sister very well because we were like two peas in a pod and we always hung out together. When I was two, my parents won a Green Card Lottery to come to the US, specifically to Fargo. They left me with my aunt and uncle because they wanted to visit America. When I was ten, they came back to get me. They had another child, my little brother. I didn't know my little brother at all, but we came back to the US as a whole family.

When I got here, it was extremely cold. It was also snowing because I came in November. On the way to our apartment, we drove on the highway and I was amazed to see snow for the first time. I always wondered what snow was like and one day when my parents went to work, I decided to jump in a pile of snow, thinking that it was going to be a little cold. However, it wasn't just cold; it was absolutely freezing.

After a couple of weeks, we went inside this huge building and they gave us a test to see what class would be the best fit for us. I took the test, and after that they told me I made it to fifth grade. I was one of the youngest in my class. Everyone was one year older than me. Class was fun, and I got into sixth grade. I had to learn different languages.

English was really difficult to learn. I didn't understand what my teachers were saying most of the time. When the teacher asked me a question in English, I knew the answer but would answer it in French, and she couldn't understand it. Overall though, classes were good and I made a lot of friends. Fargo was really different than Lomé. In Fargo, there are a lot of roads, but back in Togo, there aren't that many roads, only sand. In fact, only the capital city has roads. I was also surprised to see other building structures, such as garages. Stores here amazed me. I saw computers and huge flatscreen TVs, and that is actually how I became interested in technology. I became curious because I didn't know how such beautiful technology worked.

High school was great because I had a lot of friends with me. My French started to get worse due to lack of practice, but my English was improving, though there is still a long way to go. My favorite class is gym because it is the least work. I'm good at math, but it's not my favorite class. I love art and really enjoy drawing or doodling. I'm taking Principles of Engineering right now, and I enjoy it because I like seeing how individual structures come together and create incredible structures.

Sports are another passion of mine. During my freshman year, I played basketball and ran track, and this year I'll be playing soccer as well. I want to be goalkeeper due to my speed.

My mom used to work for a tech company here in Fargo. I don't really remember the name of the company. However, the company started laying off workers and reduced her pay more and more per month, even though she was one of the longest tenured employees. She got angry, so she quit her job. She went to Philadelphia to get to know my aunt and try to find a job, but now she currently stays at home. She eventually wants our whole family to move there. My dad currently works as a plumber and is applying for a license that will expand his practice as well as allow him to set his own work schedule. He wants to get involved in other industries such as construction, since that is what he went to college for.

I want to be a game designer because I really like drawing as well as graphic design. My eventual goal is to design my own video game. If that doesn't work out, then I'll try engineering or electrical design. I really love technology and hope to work with phones, computers, and cameras, either designing them or improving their functions.

greencardvoices.org/speakers/godwin-kouhe

Kigoma, Tanzania

Glorioza Nduwimana

From: Kigoma, Tanzania
Current City: Fargo, ND

"I LIKE MENTORING OTHER IMMIGRANT STUDENTS BECAUSE I FEEL THEIR STRUGGLE. I WENT THROUGH THE SAME STRUGGLE. I GET TO TEACH THEM HOW TO DEAL WITH PROBLEMS BECAUSE I HAVE EXPERIENCED THEM BEFORE. "

I lived in a refugee camp in Kigoma, Tanzania. My typical day consisted of waking up early to walk to school, walking home for lunch, and going back to school until around four in the afternoon. For dinner, we had to fetch wood in order to be able to cook. My parents would farm and make sure that there was enough food. My dad would also travel to go fishing so that he could sell the fish and make extra money.

Back in Africa, we were barely getting by. Food was often short in supply, and there was barely enough money left over after paying my school tuition. If you didn't have money for school, you wouldn't go to school. In short, life was difficult.

My parents were both separated from their parents in the genocide in Rwanda. That's when they went to Congo. My older brother had died during the war. They had my sister in Congo, but they didn't stay there for long. They went to Tanzania, which is where two of my siblings and I were born. That's where we stayed for twelve years until we were admitted to the US.

When I found out that I was coming to the US, I was in complete shock. I couldn't imagine myself living there at all. My perception was that the United States was only for the educated and wealthy, and I didn't think we would make it. People would say silly stuff about America like "money grows on trees" and that people walk on money and life was just a breeze. Houses were full of food and each house had its own indoor restroom, which was just unique to me. There was also this saying that Americans were going to turn African people into soft soap. Overall, I was still very excited.

Coming to the US wasn't that easy. We had to get a lot of medical checkups and physical tests and partake in many interviews to see if we were qualified. We also had to get many shots. Some of my family members and friends, including my aunts and uncles, stayed in Africa. I miss them. I hope to go back next year.

My parents had an orientation, but I didn't receive one. I didn't really have a chance to say good-bye to anyone. All I can remember is that we went to this place and stayed overnight. People were telling us that life in America wasn't going to be that easy, but I had the mindset that not everything comes easy anyway. They also told us about the benefits of living in America, specifically that if you go to school and concentrate, then you will make something out of yourself. America is the land of opportunity, and it was up to me to make something out of it.

I remember we rode in a bus to a big plane. I was very excited and kind of scared because it was my first time in a plane. I was also excited to leave Africa. Once the plane took off, we all got very scared. I don't remember the exact locations, but I know for sure that we transferred to five different flights. I remember a stop in New York where we went in an elevator. It was our first time and we cried because it was scary being crammed in a box-like structure.

First, I went to Salt Lake City, Utah. It was getting cold when we arrived in the fall of 2006. They put us in an apartment on the third floor, which was kind of scary because we were living high up and above people.

We had a person come in and tell us how to use the stove, what the bathroom was used for, and how to use other basic appliances. We were actually scared to walk around our apartment because we were afraid of disturbing others below us.

I didn't go straight to school because it was in the middle of the school year, so they gave us CDs and DVDs to learn English. We also watched TV shows and programs like PBS Kids. We had to learn how to pronounce words and how to create basic sentences. Learning English was quite difficult.

My first time at school was very difficult because the kids were a different color than I was, so I was kind of scared. However, I realized what a great opportunity the school was and how lucky I was to be able to go to a nice school. I started to tell myself that this is where my dream would start and to achieve it step by step.

There were some things that I didn't like. In particular, the food. The school kind of made me sick. I couldn't understand what other kids were saying, but when they got a translator for me, it became easier to meet other people who I eventually became friends with.

I was in Salt Lake City for nine and a half years. I moved to Fargo because my mom came and she said she really liked the environment. My dad thought that it was a great opportunity to have an adventure and came along. He also has a really good job now, and the schools here in Fargo are really good. I guess I can say that I like it here.

I like mentoring other immigrant students because I feel their struggle. I went through the same struggle. I get to teach them how to deal with problems because I have experienced them before. I also really enjoy volunteering and contributing to my community.

My favorite subject is English, but in the future I want to be a dental hygienist. I also want to be a volunteer and travel back to Africa and help where help is needed. I hope to build an orphanage back in Africa.

greencardvoices.org/speakers/glorioza-nduwimana

Jhapa, Nepal

Deo Katuwal

From: Jhapa, Nepal
Current City: Fargo, ND

"I DIDN'T KNOW HOW TO OPEN THE BATHROOM DOORS. SOME PEOPLE HELPED ME, AND I REALIZED THAT THERE WERE MANY THINGS IN THIS COUNTRY I WOULD HAVE TO LEARN ABOUT."

I was born in Jhapa, Nepal, and grew up in the camp. I liked to read, but my home was not a good environment to read in because my mother had mental problems. My mother would go many places, but she wouldn't know what she was doing. My father worked out of the country; sometimes he would go to India. He worked about twelve hours a day, but he did not make enough money to live with my family. My mother was sick and my neighbors had to give her medicine. I do not think they gave her the correct dosage of medicine because it did not work.

When I was seven or eight years old, my grandmother helped me go to school because my father was gone often and my mother was sick. My cousins also helped. They would buy me clothes that they knew I liked and they would help me get dressed.

Life in my country was difficult; many people died from different diseases. There were a lot of small houses and a big forest nearby. Many people were killed by elephants. They would go to the hospital, but there was not good care for them there. Also, there were too many sick people; children died from diseases every day.

When I was about fourteen, I worked on the roads and buildings, but they didn't pay me very much money because I was so young. I got two hundred rupees, the equivalent of two American dollars, for working ten hours.

During high school, my friend and I slept together one night. In the morning he woke up before me, at about four o'clock. When I woke up at about five, I found him hanging in the tree. He was my age, and he felt very sad about his education. He did well in every grade, but he did not get a good job, and I think that was why he died. I felt very sad.

I felt like I had to go to a new country because I needed a good education. Some people told me if I went to the United States I would have a better chance to read and write and do what I wanted to do. Some people said that going to the United States would be difficult because it is hard to understand everything. When I was sixteen, my father told me to go to the United States, but my grandmother was scared. She is seventy years old, and some neighbors told us that the country was difficult for old people. My grandmother told people not to go to the United States because she didn't know what she would do there. We stopped our process for one year after that. Then our cousins called us and we started our process to come to the United States. I lived seventeen years, nine months, twenty-seven days in the camp.

My journey to the US was difficult for me because I didn't understand English. I was so hungry, and I tried to eat the food, but I didn't like it. I ate some fries, and I liked those. I didn't know how to open the bathroom doors. Some people helped me, and I realized that there were many things in this country I would have to learn about.

We flew straight to Fargo, and my cousins came to pick us up. When I came out from the plane, I saw the whole place was white with snow. I fell down because I had the wrong shoes and clothes because I didn't know about Fargo weather. My cousin had to help me because I didn't understand how people lived in this country.

There are a lot of things I was not familiar with, such as washing machines, refrigerators, and stoves. My mother was scared of them. She was also scared of the restrooms and didn't know how to flush the water or how to clean the floors. People told me I couldn't keep my mother here because she didn't know the rules and regulations of this country.

When we were out of the house, people didn't talk with us because they thought we were new and didn't understand English. They called us, and sometimes they gave us things for our house like chairs and tables.

When I am home with my family, we speak Nepalese because my family doesn't know how to speak English. When I come to school with my friends we speak English.

When I first went to school, I didn't know how to open the lockers, but someone taught me. I liked to go to the gymnasium. I saw many of my friends playing soccer and basketball, and I wanted to play that also. They helped me play.

After that I came back to the class, and my teacher told me to do some activities. My friends understood English because they came before me, so they helped me with writing activities in class. After that I felt more comfortable.

I got a job after being here for three months. My cousin worked in the markets, and I got a job organizing food there. Many people did not know the fruit names because they were also new to the stores. In my country and other countries they have different foods and different vegetables; I wrote the name of the vegetables and helped them find their vegetables and our country's vegetables. Other times I worked in the meat area and gave meat to people.

My favorite subjects are math and history. I like to help people who are interested in reading, especially people from different countires. I also like to help them when they need food and a job and service and education.

greencardvoices.org/speakers/deo-katuwal

Texcoco, Mexico

Marai Castillo Fonseca

From: Texcoco, Mexico
Current City: Fargo, ND

"I WANT TO BE AN INTERPRETER BECAUSE FARGO IS GETTING VERY BIG AND THERE ARE A LOT OF HISPANIC PEOPLE COMING IN SO I WANT TO HELP THEM TO GET USED TO FARGO."

I was born in Mexico in a town called Texcoco. I lived with my grandma, uncle, aunt, and cousins in one small house. It was a small neighborhood, and a lot of kids lived there, so we all knew each other and went to school together. I spent a lot of time with my grandma, and I walked with her everywhere.

Then I moved to a town called San Miguel. My mother had her own photo studio there. She then started working for another company, where she met my stepfather. We moved again to another town called La Purificación; it was near San Miguel. My grandpa lived there, so we visited him a lot.

Many international people worked for my mother's company. My stepdad was in Mexico for about sixteen years, and he worked there. I think he came from Australia to work and to study. They got married, and we still live with him.

In Mexico, my mom took us to the school, then my grandma picked us up. We were at my grandma's house until my mom brought us home. What I remember a lot in Mexico is walking the streets with my friends. There were a lot of stores and street vendors. I was very different. I drew a lot in Mexico. I have notebooks of drawings. In my schools I did swimming and gymnastics.

I found out we were moving to Fargo because I asked my stepfather when his three daughters were going to visit us. I was concerned because we didn't have a lot of room in our house, but he told me that they weren't coming here. I asked him why not and he said, "We're moving." I said, "Oh, again?" and he said, "To Fargo." I didn't know what Fargo was or whether or not it even existed. I thought it was a joke because he had lived in Mexico for a long time. I asked him again, but he was serious.

Then I started looking up pictures on the Internet. I was excited because most of the pictures were of the winter, so it was very beautiful. It was going to be my first time seeing snow.

At first I was sad because I thought my pets were going to stay in Mexico. But no, they all came with us. My cat's name is Meeno. I adopted him when I was ten. There's also my stepdad's dog, Moley. When we were packing, they were very sad because they thought we were going to leave them.

When we went to the airport my grandma came with us. I was very sad because I knew I was going to miss her a lot. We flew at night. Then we arrived at Dallas. That was my first time in America. It was in an airport, but still it was in America. It was very exciting. Then I think I went to Minneapolis, and then I came to Fargo.

When I stepped out of the plane it was very windy and cold. When I came inside the airport, I was surprised because there were around twenty people in the airport and all the stores were closed. It wasn't what I was expecting at all.

When we went outside, we couldn't find the car in the wind and cold. After a while we found it. The first place where I went in Fargo was actually PetSmart because my cat and my dog were supposed to arrive hours later and I wanted to be prepared. It was very funny because I saw people with their pets walking in the store. You couldn't do that in Mexico. I was very happy when my pets arrived. I took my dog outside, my cat didn't want to, so he stayed inside. He was very scared.

We lived in an apartment at first so people could have time to put stuff in our house. We couldn't really communicate. My mom always wanted to talk to people, so I had to translate for her, but I didn't know that much English. Since my stepdad was at work all day, it was a funny experience going around and eating at various places. The food, service, and stores were all very different from what I was used to back in Mexico.

I started school two weeks after arriving in Fargo. My first day was good. I thought that people were pretending to speak English just to get me to speak English and that they really spoke Spanish. I thought that there was going to be a lot of Hispanic people here, but I was kind of the only one.

I've been here for a year and a half and my life has changed a little bit. A lot of things around me are very similar to Mexico, but the culture is very different. I still have to get used to some things. Sometimes it's still hard for me to communicate in English. I really like school here because in Mexico, the government has problems with education.

My favorite subjects in school are art and English. In middle school, I used to go to volleyball and then soccer, but now I don't do anything. I sometimes go to the gym. That's really about it.

I have a Mexican friend here. She's very nice, and we see each other a lot.

I want to go to college; I was thinking about going to Mexico but I realized that I would have better opportunities here. I want to study something along the lines of social studies. I used to be a volunteer in the Red Cross, so I really like to help people. I want to be an interpreter because Fargo is getting very big and there are a lot of Hispanic people coming in so I want to help them to get used to Fargo.

---

greencardvoices.org/speakers/marai-castillo-fonseca

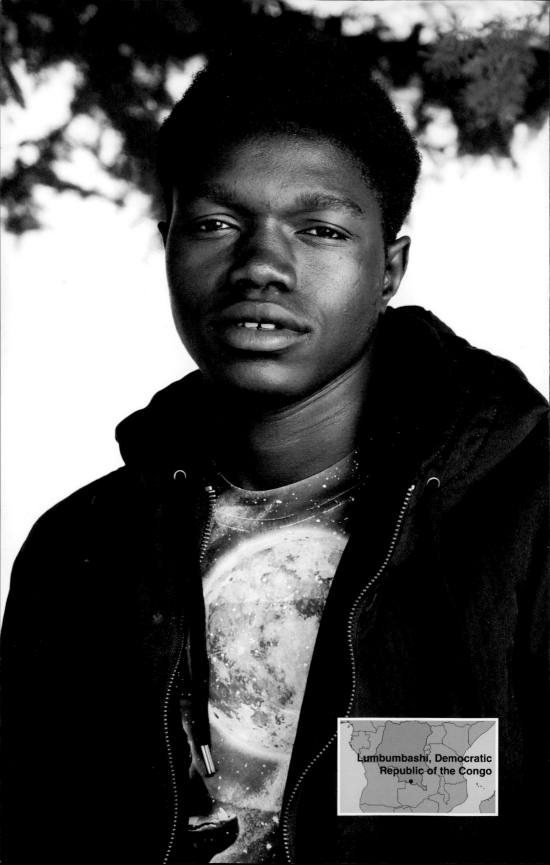

Lumbumbashi, Democratic
Republic of the Congo

Francese Manya

From: Lumbumbashi, Democratic Republic of the Congo
Current City: Fargo, ND

> "EVEN IF I GO TO AMERICA AND FIND A NICE JOB AND HAVE MONEY, I WOULDN'T HAVE ANYONE TO SHARE IT WITH BECAUSE MY MOM AND DAD ARE DEAD."

I was born in Congo in Lumbumbashi. It was kind of good where I was, but we had conflict between two tribes—Kasais and Hancomas. My grandma left us and went to Namibia, and I stayed with my mother, niece, and brothers. We were sitting in my grandma's house talking, joking, and playing outside when we just saw another tribe; they came and attacked us. They were beating my mom and my father and my brothers. We were all crying. They took a stick and they hit my head and my arm until my arm was broken and I fainted.

When I woke up, I was in the hospital and I was asking, "Where am I?" When I fainted, a neighbor picked me up and someone took me to the hospital. When I woke up, they asked me, "Do you know where you are?" And I said, "No, and why am I hurt?" And he said, "You are in the hospital. Your family was beaten, your brothers, they are dead, so we just picked you up and brought you here." He told me that my mom and dad were dead too, and they wanted to take me to my grandma.

I said, "Where is my grandma?" And they said, "She's in Namibia." I felt like asking, "Where is Namibia?" and they said, "We will take you there." From there, they just put me in the truck and took me to my grandma, who was in Namibia in a refugee camp. When I reached my grandma and she saw me, she was crying. She asked me, "Francese, what's going on?" I said, "Where we came from I saw terrible things happen to my mom and dad." And my grandma kept crying. She lost her daughter, who was my mom. I was eight years old when I started life in the camp with my grandma.

My life in the camp was so difficult. I was coming from school, and I was going to look for a job. I was hustling when I was a little kid, looking for something good for me. I had bad friends influencing me to smoke and

105

drink. My life in the camp was so hard. The camp was not that big. There was no food there, so we had to look for food and we had to work hard.

I remember that my grandma went somewhere to apply to come to the United States. My grandma said, "I'm just going there to talk with them." And I said, "Okay." One day she told me she was talking to them about how our life was and how we came from the Congo. Then they called me and asked me about my story. I told them what happened to me. I told them how I was beaten when I was a little kid and lost my mom and dad.

The day I found out that I was coming to America, my aunt called my grandma and told her that we were coming on the twenty-seventh. My grandma told us and we did not believe it. We said, "We are really going to America? No, it's not true." From there I had nothing to say. I just went into the room and started crying because I left my mom and dad.

When she said, "You are going to America," I said, "America is so far from Africa, and I left my brothers and sisters and my mom dead in Africa. Even if I go to America and find a nice job and have money, I wouldn't have anyone to share it with because my mom and dad are dead."

When we went for the check-up, they took our blood and they checked our chests. Then we went to get a plane at the airport. We got on a plane from Namibia to South Africa. After South Africa, I went to New York. After New York, I went to Chicago, and after Chicago, I came to Fargo.

When I came on the plane, I was so excited but kind of afraid too. The way you see America on the TV, people are playing around, but when I came it was not that way, it was so different. A lot of things were different. Places and rules were different. Rules are different in America compared to where I came from. Stores are different and money is so complicated. And there are banks.

I started school last month, and I made new friends. I met new teachers, and I'm playing soccer now for South High School. I scored three goals. If I finish high school, I want to go to college to be a scientist in the future. It would be a good career for me; in school I like science and I like knowing a lot about things.

One of the things that I like here is walking. I also like school here. I work at Taco Bell. I just started working there last week. The people are so good there. The manager is good. I work hard too. My life is going alright now.

I live now with my grandma and my cousin, and everything is going well. School is kind of good too. I like my friends. Everything is perfect now.

greencardvoices.org/speakers/francese-manya

Nairobi, Kenya

Sowda Shube

From: Nairobi, Kenya
Current City: Fargo, ND

> "I LIKE STANDING UP FOR PEOPLE AND TELLING AND SHOWING OTHERS THAT THEY HAVE RIGHTS AND THEY CAN DO WHAT THEY FEEL EVEN IF IT IS A LITTLE CONTROVERSIAL. "

I was born in Nairobi. We lived in a small town called Kakuma. It is kind of a refugee camp, but we built our own houses. I lived with my parents and my siblings. I had two younger sisters, and we had a grandma, aunts, and uncles. When we were in Nairobi, they lived with us. We used to go to Nairobi and stay for a couple months, but eventually we had to go back to Kakuma for the immigration process.

We made our houses very small; they were made out of sticks and mud. They were almost like huts. We put sandbags by the door so the house wouldn't get flooded when it rained. We didn't have problems with food or anything like that because my dad used to work with the buses, so he was paid on a regular basis and we were pretty well off. We had Somali food like sambusas, mandazi, rice, and pasta.

The weather was really hot sometimes. When people in Fargo say, "Oh my God it's really hot and it's like 100 degrees" I'm like, "It's nothing compared to where I was when I was younger." It would get as hot as 120 degrees sometimes. Right after the weather was really hot, it would rain all of the sudden. It would be heavy rain, and because we were literally in the middle of two rivers, we would experience terrible flooding.

I used to go to school right by my house. I'd wake up around 4:30 in the morning, and I would pray and read the Quran because I'd have to know what I was reading and memorize it. We'd pray five times a day. We didn't do anything in the house, so we memorized the Quran and we had to read two pages a day. I'd wake up really early because if I didn't, I'd get punished.

At 6:00 a.m. sharp, I needed to be at school. I wore regular cultural clothes and a big hijab. I would just wear a dress or something under it. I'd go and stay there until 9:00, and then they'd let me go to breakfast. Breakfast was around 9:30, and I'd have about an hour before I came back. Then I had classes from 10:30 until 2:00 because that's the second time we pray.

After I prayed, I would have a three-hour break, so I did my own things until 5:00, when I had to pray again. After that, we would be at the school practicing different parts of the culture and reading the Quran. I had a few friends, and we'd always be in groups and read together. At 7:00 p.m., the entire school prayed together, and then school was done. We had Fridays and Saturdays off, because Friday is a day of worship in Muslim culture.

We came to America in January of 2009, but I remember, two years before that, when my dad would wait for the news every day. There was a board downtown, and if your name was on it then you would be able to go to America. I remember every day my dad would go down there and check to see if our names were there. After a year he just kind of quit.

I remember one night when we were all together and my dad was coming home from work. My uncle came running, and my mom was making dinner for us. We're all getting ready to eat and sleep and my uncle said, "Oh my God, you guys are on the board!" My mom didn't believe it because my dad had given up on that. We went to go check, and we were actually there. Unfortunately, it was really sad when I told my friends because I thought I would never see them again. I remember one of my little cousins asking if I could put him in a suitcase and take him with me. I felt really sad but, ironically, they all came to America eventually and actually some of them now go to Davies High School. It was a sad moment, but it was exciting at the same time. I was unsure about going someplace that I didn't know.

We took a plane from Nairobi, but I don't remember to where exactly. I remember the first plane would go all the way up in the air and come back down, and it felt like I was falling and like I was going to throw up. I felt so sick and I thought I was the only one who felt sick since it was the first time I had been on a plane. The next day we took another plane, and that was better. I slept through the whole thing, and after another flight we got to Chicago.

I lived in Chicago for a month and a half. I remember our house wasn't ready, so we stayed with a host family. The mother was a really nice person. She had a daughter, two sons, a husband, and a dog. She hosted a lot of families, and one day she had a big feast for all of us. She cooked a feast with my mom and another lady she'd hosted, and we all sat and ate together.

Honestly, when I first got to Fargo, I hated it because when I was in Chicago, I stayed in my house and did nothing. When we got to Fargo, we were always going to hospitals and schools. I went to Kennedy Elementary School, and I remember the first time I went there it was snowing really hard and there was ice all the way up to my knees. I told my dad that I hated the cold, and he told me that everything was going to work out. My teacher was great, all the students were really nice to me, and I even met a girl who spoke Swahili. She translated most things for me and was able to help me around the school. All my teachers were willing to help me, especially my ELL teachers. I had four ELL teachers, and they were really kind to me and taught me a lot of new stuff. I don't know what I would have done without them.

My life has changed a lot. My dad and I have jobs, and my mom stays at home. I play soccer, volleyball, and basketball. I work at a retirement home right now. Everyone there is great. We have plenty of diversity, even at work.

The school helps a lot, too. The staff, students, and principal are all great. I work Tuesdays and Thursdays after school, and other days I just come home and cook for my parents. I help out around the house, and if I'm not working that day I will go to the gym, since basketball and soccer seasons are just around the corner.

My grandma and my aunt have lived together since they came here in 2006. They used to live in Seattle. My grandma, her father, and my father got their citizenships around the same time. She lives with us now, but her family is back in Africa. She went to Sweden to see her sister. She's actually coming back tomorrow, and she's probably going to live with us for another year because we are planning on moving to Minneapolis.

I'm trying to become a lawyer. All my teachers tell me that I talk a lot and that I am good at arguing. I really like making people feel comfortable around me, so being a lawyer would be a great job for me. I also want to let people know that they have freedom of speech. I like standing up for people and telling and showing others that they have rights and they can do what they feel even if it is a little controversial.

greencardvoices.org/speakers/sowda-shube

Morang, Nepal

Nobin Gurung

From: Morang, Nepal
Current City: Fargo, ND

> "WE WENT TO A BIG HOTEL WHERE WE JUST STARED FROM THE WINDOW AND LOOKED AT THE TALL BUILDINGS. CARS WERE DRIVING BY AND IT WAS PRETTY AMAZING TO SEE NEW CARS AND BIG BUILDINGS IN AMERICA."

I was born in Nepal in a refugee camp called Pathari Camp. My life was miserable because we didn't have lot of money. The food we got was rations given to us from the government. We used to get twenty-five kilograms of rice per family. We had to go to a school that was built with bamboos and bricks. But I had fun with my friends and played soccer.

In 2007, my dad left me to go work in India, and he lived there for three years. He didn't contact us, so we thought that our father was lost. It was difficult to live life in a refugee camp without him. If he would have been there, then he could have made money and been able to feed us.

After three years, he came back to Nepal. He didn't come to meet us, but instead he went to a place called Beni. It's the middle of Nepal. He went there and stayed for three more years, and after that, he finally contacted us saying that he was going to meet us. We were excited to meet him.

After he got to Morang and eventually to our refugee camp, I saw him with another wife, and I was shocked. In fact, the whole family was shocked. He asked us to go with him and study in private school, but we didn't want to go because we had lots of friends in the refugee camp. So my dad reluctantly gave us his signature to come to the US instead.

We waited for one or two years until we finally got the call telling us that we were going to the US. We had to do medical check-ups for the process to get started. After one month, we got to the date of our departure. We went from Pathari Camp to Chandragadhi on a bus. We went to Chandragadhi airport, and then we got on plane to Kathmandu on January 24, 2014.

It was pretty amazing, but I was terrified because it was my first time on a plane. We stayed in Kathmandu for three days. In Kathmandu I found friends from different camps in Nepal. We had fun playing cards and other

113

games together.

After three days, we had to leave Kathmandu and get on a plane to Hong Kong. After three or four hours in Hong Kong, we flew to California. When we got there we were really sick and vomiting. We had to stay there overnight because we missed the connecting flight. We went to a big hotel where we just stared from the window and looked at the tall buildings. Cars were driving by and it was amazing to see new cars and big buildings in America.

The next morning we went to the airport to fly to Fargo. Once we got to there, we saw a lot of white people talking in English. I could understand some words, but not all of them. It was pretty difficult.

My cousin, Bir, was waiting for us at the airport. He came to Fargo in 2012. Once we got outside of the airport, it was very cold and snowing. The snow was about three inches high. We didn't have very warm jackets because we didn't know that it would be snowing in Fargo.

I remember a lot of things about the first time I went to his apartment. The apartment smelled bad and I thought it was big, but after staying there with a lot of people it didn't feel that big anymore. There were African and American people walking down the stairs. We were kind of confused because we didn't understand living in an apartment. I didn't know there would be a lot of people living in the apartment; it was different than what I was used to. It was a higher standard of living, way better than our camp. The apartments were built with good materials, unlike in our camp.

When I first went to Carl Ben Eielson Middle School, it was different than school in the camp. There were people yelling during lunch. We had to eat lunch in the school, but in refugee camp we had a one-hour break to go home and eat lunch. There were a lot of people, some of them were Nepalese. I didn't talk to them because it was my first day and I didn't know English.

Students made fun of me, and it was really bad. After a month or so, I got used to it and I started making a lot of friends. I had American, Nepalese, and African friends. I learned English by talking to my friends; we would talk about random things and tell stories.

After school, I used to play soccer with friends at Orange Park, a small soccer field. There were Mexican people who used to come and play with us and speak their language. We couldn't understand what they were saying, but we still tried to speak English with them. That's another way I learned English.

My older brother is a junior at South High. My younger brother is ten years old; he is in fifth grade at Jefferson School. I have my mom with me, and she works at a Holiday Inn as a housekeeper. Now I'm a freshman at Fargo South High. It is way different than middle school. You get a lot of homework and have a lot of things to do. I play soccer for Fargo South High. I am on the Junior Varsity team and I am on the Varsity reserve. My favorite subjects are math and science because they're fun. My after school activity is mostly soccer. I want to study cardiology.

greencardvoices.org/speakers/nobin-gurung

Dodoma, Tanzania

Iraguha Yvette

From: Dodoma, Tanzania
Current City: Fargo, ND

"MY HOPE IS THAT PEOPLE IN AMERICA GET TO KNOW OUR MOTHERLAND, AFRICA, MORE AS WE ARE LEARNING ABOUT THEIR LAND. "

I was born in Tanzania, Africa. My parents were born in Rwanda. They moved to Burundi; then they moved to Tanzania. That's where they had me and my other sister. I had one younger sister at that time. Another sister was born when we were to coming to America. Another one was born here in Fargo.

What I remember about my country is it was a beautiful country. There were many people. I had things to do. I remember going to the forest with my friends, playing a game called "jolo-holo." That's what I remember mostly.

I went to school but not that much because every time I went to school I had to move to other cities.

I lived in this little town and we had a lot of land and two shops. We had a big house with a big garden. When I was nine years old, people started to threaten us. They wanted money. So one day they broke into our house. My sister, my cousin, my parents, and I were sleeping. We did not know they were going to target us.

That night someone knocked on our door and claimed that they were our neighbor, but they were not. So my dad opened the door. They said, "Put your hands up." One thing they did not know is that my mom had already run away. We were still asleep. They came to check if my mom was with us while we were sleeping. They took all the money. After a few months, they broke in again and poisoned the food. They wanted my dad to die because he was the wrong tribe. Where I lived in Burundi, they did not like Rwandese people.

Then we went to the refugee camp, but those people were still looking for us. Then we applied for immigration. Since my dad was well known, they did it fast, and we came to Fargo, North Dakota. We don't know if they are

117

still looking for us. We are scared to go back to our own country, but one day we will.

On the day my parents said we were going to America, I was scared and nervous because it was a big change for me. We didn't tell anyone because people were trying to kill us. We just packed our stuff and went.

My journey was scary and I was nervous because it was my first time seeing white people. Because where I used to live in Africa, we used to get one white person visiting the town. I was nervous seeing all the white people around me.

I did not eat anything on the plane because it looked nasty. The only thing I drank was pop because it tasted sweet and it was my first time drinking it.

We arrived on April 12, 2010. It was cold and freezing. It was my first time experiencing that kind of environment because what I was used to was a warm, normal temperature.

It was my first time seeing an airport and a lot of people traveling. It was my first time riding an escalator and I was scared, so I used the stairs to climb down. We took a cab to come to our new house and everything looked nice. It was my first time having that kind of nice house. The one thing that scared me was the toilet.

When I first got here, we went to our house and found there were a stove, a sink, and a bathroom with a tub. All that was new to me. Because back there we didn't have all that. It was a different style. We had the kitchen, sink, and bathroom outside the house.

When I first came in April, I went to school only for a couple months because the school was almost closing for summer. I was scared because there were a lot of white kids. At the school I went to there were no black people in my class, so I was scared and nervous. Some kids bullied me because I didn't know the language and I looked different from them.

The following year I had this teacher; her name was Mrs. Fortun. She helped me a lot. She taught me English and many things that I needed to know. So my school year was a little bit better.

My life right now is boring because I don't get to do many things I used to do in Africa, like play my favorite games, hang out with my friends, and go to the forest.

My hobby is singing. I love singing, dancing, and cooking. Last Friday I just went to Williston, North Dakota. We were there for a performance.

I sing in a church choir, but we don't travel that much unless someone invites us. That's when we go. My favorite song is in Swahili. It's called "Ni naenda kwa baba" (I Am Going to the Father). Another one in English is called "Above All Kings. "

My hope is that people in America get to know our motherland, Africa, more as we are learning about their land. My dream is to become a fashion designer. But I am not very sure that's what I want to do. I have many years to go, so I have many years to figure out what I want.

greencardvoices.org/speakers/iraguha-yvette

Tessenei, Eritrea

Osman Osman

From: Tessenei, Eritrea
Current City: Fargo, ND

> "I CAN'T CHANGE HOW PEOPLE TREAT ME OR WHAT THEY SAY TO ME. ONLY I CAN CHANGE HOW I REACT TO THAT."

I am from Eritrea, which is located on horn of Africa. It shares borders with Ethiopia, Djibouti, Sudan, Yemen, and the Red Sea. Eritrea is a country that gained its independence from Ethiopia in 1991. I am from the tribe Belin, and we lived in the highlands of Eritrea.

I was born and raised in Tessenei. It is in the west of Eritrea and close to the border of Sudan. I went to an Arabic school in Tessenei.

My life was pretty good. My mom was somewhat of a handcrafter and a designer of clothes, and she mostly made Chinese clothes and dresses.

The government, however, worsened our lives because they put a lot of taxes on my mother's shop and then took her license away. From that point on, there was no income for her, so I was forced to drop out of school in eighth grade and work.

I worked as a donkey cart driver. The government was searching for smugglers because there was a lot of contraband near the border of Eritrea. At that time, they accused me of being a smuggler because of my friend. He was older than me and was a merchant. He had a job transferring goods from Eritrea to Sudan and vice versa.

One day, when I was fifteen years old, I was watching soccer in a recreation club called the Barka and the government broke into our home in the middle of the night. When I came home, my mother told me there were state security officers who came looking for me. In Eritrea, there are no warnings before they break into your home because the police can do whatever they want.

The officers left because they couldn't find me. They told my mother to bring me to them, so they could put me in jail. My mother, however, refused to do so. I went to my friend's house and I stayed there for two days.

After that, I decided to leave the country because if they caught me, I would be executed for sure.

I left by myself and moved to the city of Kassala, Sudan. I lived in the district of Mourabit, where I started to work in a cafeteria. Around December of 2012, my friend introduced me to some of his friends who ran a mining pit. They promised us a lot of pay to go work for them, so we agreed. Unfortunately, it was a big trick. After traveling for three hours in a pickup with all of our stuff, they stopped the car and they pointed guns at us.

They sprayed our eyes with a chemical substance and they blindfolded us. We traveled for seven days, crossing two countries. I didn't know exactly where we were, but I knew it was in Egypt. When we finally stopped, we were forced into a cave. There was another group with nineteen people of different nationalities all in the back of the cave. They asked me for a SIM card and number to call my parents for ransom money. I didn't want them to contact my family, so I gave them a random number. They took my cell phone, my laptop, and my money. They checked, but they didn't find any numbers.

They tortured me with electricity and various other methods. I still have knee problems to this day because they struck me with the back of a Kalashnikov. The muscle in my leg was also damaged. I spent around forty-five days with them. We ate only one time each day, usually bread with cheese but no water.

We slept in a cave in the night, outside, and it was very, very cold. It was like Fargo. They came to me and insisted that I pay the ransom. First they asked for $4,000. Then they raised it to $10,000, and then to $15,000. I couldn't pay $15,000. Other people did pay $15,000 and then they released them. Soon I thought of a plan and just told them, "Ok, give me some time. I can pay. I'm going to."

One day I got the chance to escape, but I was scared because there were armed people outside. They were doing cocaine and hashish with a hookah. They told me that if I didn't pay, then they would take my kidney.

That night, the guard was drunk and fell asleep. Since I was only tied up with cloth, I decided to escape. I wanted to bring the lady who was tied to me along, but I thought she would scream and make noise, so I didn't wake her. After I took off the cloth ties, I went outside and took the guard's shoes. I put the shoes on backwards so that they would think that I went the other direction. This gave me time.

I traveled four hours to a reach a village. I was scared the village people were the same tribe as my kidnappers. They were Bedouins. There was no choice, because I was weak and had not eaten or showered for forty-five days. I found an old man in a grocery store. I told him what happened because I spoke Arabic. Surprisingly, he took me to his house. I was still careful not to trust him, and I was very tense. I spent two days with him in his house, and I took a shower and ate some food. He told me that he couldn't do anything for me there, but he said he would help me get to Cairo, Egypt. It was about seven hundred miles away.

He found someone to accompany me, and he gave me fifty pounds of Egyptian money. So, I went to Cairo with that man. In Cairo, I felt lost and I didn't know where to go. The first thing I did was to go to a shop and get my hair cut. Then, I bought a T-shirt. Eventually, I went to the Metro subway and I spent the whole night going from one station to another.

I met a British man named Mohamed who knew about a place that helped people like me. He told me that I should register with an organization called AMERA. So I went to AMERA and they registered me as someone who needed help. They assigned me an apartment in a place called Dugi.

I applied to the United Nations for asylum and for an ID card. Before that, I didn't have an identity. Nothing showed who I was.

At that time, I was depressed, overwhelmed, and frustrated, but life in Egypt gradually became better. The people and language became more familiar to me. Since I spoke Arabic, I just had to learn the accent. Soon some people started a revolution against the Egyptian government. All my time was spent in the apartment because there was shooting outside, so people did not go outside for weeks.

After that my immigration process through the United Nations started. They called me and told me that I had been accepted to go to America. It took three months to finish the process. I was very excited for the new opportunity.

When I landed in Fargo, it was cold. It was wintertime, but it did not bother me. I like Fargo because it is a small and quiet city.

When I started high school, I remember being in gym class. I hadn't played basketball before, so when we played in the gym, I kicked it with my foot. Some kid said, "Whatcha doing?" I said, "My name is not whatcha, my name is Osman." They said, "No, we don't mean that's your name, we mean what are you doing?" It was very confusing for me.

In high school, there were not many people from my country. I only had a few friends. Some people made fun of me because of the color of my skin and my accent. They bullied me, but I didn't care. I can't change how people treat me or what they say to me. I can only change how I react to that. I can turn away from the stupid people.

Now, I live with foster parents. They have two daughters and two sons. They are nice, but I really want to be with my brother and my real family. No one likes being a refugee. I hate being a refugee. I don't like how people say bad things about refugees. I am not bad. I want do well here in America.

I can't go back to my country, because I left the country when the government was looking for me. My mother and brother have since moved to Sudan. I hope to reunite with them someday. I also hope to study something related to biology or medicine so I can help people.

---

greencardvoices.org/speakers/osman-osman

Hanoi, Vietnam

Van Tran

From: Hanoi, Vietnam
Current City: Fargo, ND

> "I WAS NERVOUS BECAUSE THAT WAS THE FIRST TRIP I WENT ON WITHOUT MY MOM AND MY DAD AND EVERYTHING WAS SO NEW FOR ME...THAT TRIP WAS DIFFICULT."

I was born in Hanoi, the capital city of Vietnam. I always had to wake up at six thirty a.m. to get ready for school, and classes started at seven thirty. If I woke up late, I got stuck in the traffic jam and I would smell a lot of smoke from cars and motorbikes. I used to play basketball with my friend, and we won a lot of prizes.

My family has four people: my mom, my dad, my older sister, and me. I liked it in Hanoi because I have a lot of memories of my family from there, like going to beaches and to other countries and eating a lot of food together.

I moved here because my mom's family moved to Fargo. There was a war in Guangzhou, China, so they had to move to the US. My mom wanted me to live with them. She told me to go to the US and live with my grandma because the US provided better education and there was no air pollution. That's why we moved here.

One day after school she said, "Van, now you will go to high school in the US." I just said, "Whoa, okay." I was very excited because when I was little kid, I always dreamt about going to the US and studying because the US has no air pollution and a lot of cars, and I love cars. They also teach basketball really well, and I play basketball, so I was very excited about that.

On that day I had to say good-bye to my mom and dad. It was the seventh of July. After that I went to the US with my sister. The whole trip took nearly the whole day. I had to transfer onto different flights in Tokyo and Chicago. The longest trip was from Tokyo to Chicago, which took about fifteen hours. My back was hurting because we couldn't lie down. If I lay down, the person behind me yelled and asked why I was so rude.

I was nervous because that was the first trip I went on without my mom and my dad and everything was so new for me. At that time my English was not good, so when people said things to me I would just reply with confusion. That trip was difficult.

My mom's family was waiting for me. When I got to the airport, they were sitting outside and waiting and waving at me because that was the first time I'd seen them in America. I hadn't seen them for about ten years. Everyone was excited to see my sister and me. They said, "Oh my God, you look much prettier than you did in Vietnam," and "You are much bigger," and "You have changed since I saw you in Vietnam."

The day after I came to Fargo, it snowed, so I couldn't go outside. That day, the temperature was just around ten or fifteen degrees, but the lowest temperature it got in Vietnam was around fifty degrees. Our bodies weren't adapted to that temperature, so I stayed home and all my mom's family came to my grandma's house and visited me and gave me a lot of presents.

When the weather was a little bit warmer I went outside with my auntie. She took me to the supermarket and Wal-Mart and other similar stores. That day I wore a lot of layers: sweatshirt, shoes, boots, and jeans. However, everyone else I saw was just wearing T-shirts and a hoodie, and I was just like, "What? How can our body adapt to that temperature?" I was dressed like a panda, and they were wearing what I would normally wear on a sunny day in Vietnam.

This is my first year of school in America. I was kind of nervous and kind of worried because the high schools in the Hollywood movies I'd seen had lots of bullying, and I was like, "Am I going to be bullied or what?" I was also nervous that they would teach something and I wouldn't understand them and they would get angry because they would have to repeat themselves.

It was not like what I expected. I thought that everyone was going to bully me, but they were very friendly to me, and they just kept talking to me until I understood what they were talking about.

My life now is amazing because people here are friendly and they help me with difficult situations, like how to do a specific homework problem or how to write. I live with my grandma, and it's pretty cool because my grandma always cooks for us and it's delicious. My family is very friendly, and they took me to visit Minneapolis. After school, I always play basketball with my friends. It's kind of easy and not difficult like I had expected.

My mom moved here recently but my dad is not here because he works for the country and can't move out.

My dream is to graduate from high school and go to NDSU to study accounting because I want become an accountant. My mom also says that if I do accounting I will know how to support myself and be financially stable, which is what my mom wants. I also love math, so would help me with accounting. I want to be an accountant so I know how to support myself, and I want to learn to control my income and help my parents get out of their miserable conditions.

greencardvoices.org/speakers/van-tran

Mogadishu, Somalia

Zakariye Muhudin Abdulle

From: Mogadishu, Somalia
Current City: Fargo, ND

> "WHEN I FINISH HIGH SCHOOL, I WANT TO STUDY I.T. AT COLLEGE OR BECOME A SOCCER PLAYER. ANYTHING IS POSSIBLE, RIGHT?"

I was born in Mogadishu, Somalia. I lived mostly in a boarding school. The daily ritual would usually be waking up, eating breakfast, going to school, eating lunch, more classes, eating dinner, and going to sleep at the school.

We had three days per month when we could go home and see our family. I usually saw my mother, father, and siblings, and we sat around, ate, and didn't do anything extraordinary.

We moved to Malaysia when I was eleven. We moved because of the constant fighting in Somalia. Lots of people were dying everyday, and life was really unstable. My father was the first to want to leave. My mother later decided that it was unsafe in Somalia, so we moved to Malaysia.

I remember stopping in Dubai on the way to Malaysia. I was in the airport for eleven days because I'd lost my passport. My family went ahead of me so I spent the time wandering around the airport and sleeping on the floor. My parents didn't know any English, so they couldn't ask the authorities in Malaysia for help, and I didn't know any English either. I couldn't communicate with anyone in the airport. It was really scary and difficult for us. Luckily, we had some family friends who were able to assist me and locate my parents. When I finally got to Malaysia, my parents were relieved because we were reunited again.

I lived in Kuala Lumpur, the capital of Malaysia. I went to school there for two years, and I enjoyed it. It was a little different than school in Somalia. If you were late to school, you had to pay money to get in, and if you didn't have the money then they would send you back home.

I enjoyed the school more because it wasn't a boarding school, so I was able to see my family more often. I hung out with my brothers, sisters, and friends, and on weekends we would usually go on a trip. We would go

131

someplace, sleep there, and then come back late Sunday night because school started early on Monday.

My father was a teacher in Somalia, so he was able to pay for the basics for my family. When we first got to Malaysia, he couldn't find a job, and that was difficult. My mom also couldn't find a job because she had never really worked before. It was a struggle since they had to support us. After a few months, they both managed to find jobs.

My mom worked in a restaurant, and my dad worked for a Somali school in Malaysia. It was a school for little kids, so I went to a Malaysian school. Sometimes the pay wasn't enough, so my dad had to ask the school for extra time or extra stipend, since we were refugees. The schools were nice enough to either pay for half of the payments or grant my father an extra month's pay.

I was in school for two years, and that's where I picked up the Malaysian language. It was really a tool I needed for survival. If I wanted to buy something, I had to speak their language, since I didn't know any English and they didn't really know any Somali. I ended up translating and helping my family whenever they needed to speak Malaysian.

When we found out we were going to the US, we were really happy because those five years in Malaysia had been difficult. We quickly made preparations and headed for the airport.

We arrived at the airport at night, but we hadn't slept the night before because we wanted to sleep on the airplane. My younger brother Yaya got lost. Since we hadn't eaten or slept much, he was tired and hungry. I wasn't paying attention, and then suddenly he was gone. We thought he went to get food, and when he didn't return, we searched for him at the restaurants. An hour later, we found him sleeping in a random location.

We finally got our flight and we went from Malaysia to Japan, Japan to New York, New York to Minneapolis, and Minneapolis to Fargo. I was scared of the airplane, so I didn't get much sleep.

I came here on April 1, and it was still too cold for my family. When we got to Fargo, it was night so I didn't realize how cold it was. When I woke up the next morning, I ate breakfast and went outside to play some soccer. When I went outside I was wearing a big jacket but others around me were only wearing T-shirts. They found the way I dressed funny and warned me that the real cold comes when the snow arrives.

When I first started school, it was bad because I didn't have a lot of friends and I didn't know much English. I was overwhelmed by the size of the school. The hallways were confusing, and I didn't know where my classes were. I was often late to class and was unable to tell the teacher that the reason I was late was because I was lost.

Now my life is very good. I have a lot of friends in school and in soccer. I understand a lot more English, though there are still a few words and phrases that I'm not sure about. Overall, I would say that I am very happy.

When I finish high school, I want to study IT in college or become a soccer player. Anything is possible, right?

---

greencardvoices.org/speakers/zakariye-muhudin-abdulle

Afterword

Learning from the students' stories in this book is just the beginning. The more important work starts when we engage in difficult but necessary conversations about the changing face of our nation.

Immigration plays a significant role in modern America; one in five Americans speak a language other than English at home. From classrooms to bookclubs, from the individual interested in learning more about his immigrant neighbor to the business owner looking to understand her employees and business partners, this book is an important resource for all Americans.

For these reasons, we have included a portion of our Act4Change study guide, a glossary, and links to the students' video narratives, intended to expand the impact of these students' journeys to the United States. The Act4Change study guide is an experiential learning tool. It promotes participation scaffolded with thoughtful discussion questions and activities that are designed for hands-on learning, emphasizing personal growth. It will help teachers, students, and all participants examine their own stories.

We hope to spark deeply meaningful conversations about identity, appreciation of difference, and our shared human experience.

If you would like an extended version of the study guide or to learn about educator workshops on how to use the Act4Change study guide, visit our website—*www.greencardvoices.org.*

Act4Change:
A Green Card Voices Study Guide

Each person has the power to tell their own story in their own voice. The art of storytelling translates across cultures and over time. In order to learn about and appreciate voices other than our own, we must be exposed to and given tools to foster an understanding of a variety of voices. We must be able to view the world from others' perspectives in order to act as agents of change in today's world.

Green Card Youth Voices is comprised of the inspirational voices from a young group of recent immigrants to the US that can be shared with a wide audience. This study guide will provide readers with questions to help them explore universal themes, such as storytelling, immigration, identity, and perspective.

Introduce New Voices:
Participants will select one of the thirty storytellers featured in *Green Card Youth Voices* and adopt that person's story as their own "new voice." For example, one participant may choose Mesaged Abakar while another might choose Nobin Gurung. Participants will become familiar with the life story of their "new voice" and develop a personal connection to it. After each participant has chosen his or her "new voice," read the personal essay first and then watch the video.

Act4Change 1 :
Answer the following questions—
1. Why did you select the storyteller that you did?
2. What was interesting to you about his/her story?
3. What do you and the storyteller have in common?
4. What have you learned as a result of reading/listening to this person's story?

Learn About New Voices 1:

Divide participants into groups of three or four people. Provide each group with copies of the written narratives from five selected stories. Each person within each group will read one of the five narratives. Once finished, the participants will share their narratives with the others. Then, as a group, choose one of the five "voices" and watch that person's video.

Afterward, go on to the journal activity below.

Act4Change 2:

Answer the following questions—

1. What new information about immigrants did you learn from this second storyteller?
2. Compare and contrast the storyteller's video to his/her story. Which did you prefer? Why?
3. What are some similarities between you and the second storyteller?
4. If this really was your "new voice," what might you want to know about America upon arriving?
5. If you could only bring one suitcase on your move to another country, what would you pack in it? Why?

Learn About New Voices 2:

Each participant will be given a third "new voice," and only one can go to each student; there can be no duplicates.

Inform participants not to share the identity of their "new voice." Participants will try to match their classmates' "new voices" to one of the stories in the book. Encourage participants to familiarize themselves with all of the voices featured in *Green Card Youth Voices.*

Act4Change 3:

1. After they are given their "new voice," ask participants to try and create connections between this third voice and themselves. Have the students read their story and then watch the video of their "new voice." Have them think of a piece of art, dance, song, spokenword, comic, sculpture, or other medium of their choosing that best describes their "new voice."

2. Participants will present a 3-5 minute artistic expression for the larger group from the perspective of their "new voice" in thirty-five minutes. The audience will have a template with a chart that includes each of the thirty GCYV students' names, their photo, and a one- or two-sentence abbreviated biography[1]. Audience members will use this chart throughout the activities to keep track of what has been learned about each voice that they have heard.

3. Ask the participants to describe the relationship between the Green Card Youth Voices and themselves:

    a. What did you notice about the form of artistic expression and the story?

    b. What drew you to this specific art form?

    c. Do you notice any cultural relationships between the "new voice" and the piece of art that was chosen?

    d. What is your best advice to immigrant students on how to succeed in this country? State? City?

---

1. Visit the Green Card Voices website for templates.

More than Meets the Eye:

In small groups, have participants read and watch three or four selected narratives from *Green Card Youth Voices*. After that, have group members tell each other facts about themselves and tell the others in the group what they would not know just by looking at them. For example, participants can share an interesting talent, a unique piece of family history, or a special interest. Then have group members discuss things that they found surprising about the students in *Green Card Youth Voices*.

Think about the "new voice" you transformed in Act4Change 3. Tell your group something that was "more than meets the eye" from the perspective of that "new voice!"

For the complete version of Act4Change: A Green Card Voices Study Guide, visit our website—www.greencardvoices.org

See also:

Act4Change: A Green Card Youth Voices Study Guide, Workshop for Educators
This workshop is a focused learning experience crafted to deepen teacher understanding and provide instructional strategy, particularly designed to be used in conjunction with *Green Card Youth Voices*.

Glossary

AMERA-Egypt: A branch of AMERA UK (Africa and Middle East Refugee Assistance United Kingdom), a charity registered in the UK that provides legal assistance and representation for asylum seekers concerning their refugee status with the United Nations High Commissioner for Refugees (UNHCR).

Bedouin: An Arabic word that is used commonly to refer to the people (Arab and non-Arab) who live, or have descended from tribes who lived stationary or nomadic lifestyles outside cities and towns (living primarily in the Middle Eastern deserts, especially North Africa and the Arabian peninsula).

caseworker: A person appointed to oversee the status of a refugee.

cochlear implant: An electronic medical device that replaces certain functions of the ear, implanted into the ear.

contraband: Goods or merchandise whose trade and/or possession is forbidden.

Dhagana: A village in the Punjab state in India.

DV (Diversity Visa): The Diversity Immigrant Visa Program (DV Program) makes up to fifty thousand immigrant visas available annually, drawn from a random selection among all entries to individuals who are from countries with low rates of immigration to the United States. The DV Program is administered by the US Department of State (DOS). Commonly called the Green Card Lottery, it is a United States congressionally mandated lottery program for receiving a United States Permanent Resident Card (also referred to as a "green card").

Dzongkha: Also known as Bhutanese, the official language of Bhutan

ESL/ELL/EL: English as a Second Language/English Language Learner/English Learner— all words to describe English language study programs for nonnative speakers.

forms: Grade or a class of students in a school. A term typically used in the United Kingdom and former British colonies. First form, or form 1, is the equivalent of seventh grade in the US.

fufu: a staple food in many countries of West Africa and the Caribbean. It is often made with cassava and green plantain flour.

green card: A commonly used name for a Lawful Permanent Resident Card, an identification card attesting to the permanent resident status of an immigrant in the United States. The green card serves as proof that its holder, a Lawful Permanent Resident (LPR), has been officially granted immigration benefits, which include permission to reside and take employment in the United States. Green card also refers to an immigration process of becoming a permanent resident.

Green Card Lottery: See "Diversity Visa Lottery" above.

hashish: A cannabis-related drug that is typically smoked.

hookah: A type of pipe used for smoking tobacco.

injera: An East African sourdough flatbread with a spongy texture.

IOM: The International Organization for Migration.

IT: Information Technology.

jolo-holo: A children's game in Tanzania.

Kalashnikov: A type of machine gun.

Kiganda: Also known as Luganda, a language spoken in Uganda.

Kirundi: A language spoken by people from Burundi and parts of Tanzania, Congo, and Uganda.

Krahn: A language spoken by the Krahn ethnic group of Liberia and the Ivory Coast.

LSS (Lutheran Social Services): The primary refugee resettlement agency in Fargo, ND. LSS has offices all across the United States.

mandazi: A type of fried bread popular in East Africa.

orientation (in refugee camps): Education on the customs of a country, in this case the US.

PetSmart: An American retail chain that provides products for pets.

pillage: To rob using violence.

Red Cross (American Red Cross): A social service organization that responds with emergency relief internationally, usually in the form of medical aid.

refugee: A person who is outside their country of residence or nationality who is unable or unwilling to return and unable and unwilling to avail herself or himself of the protection of their original country of residence or nationality because of persecution or a well-founded fear of persecution on account of race, religion, nationality, membership in a particular social group, or political opinion.

refugee camp: Temporary housing for people displaced by warfare or religious or political reasons.

SIM card: a portable memory chip used in most cell phones.

sambusa (alt. sombusa): A fried food filled with savory ingredients such as potatoes, peas, and spices.

UN employees: People that are employed by the United Nations.

Upward Bound: A pre-college program designed to help prepare high school students for higher education.

visa: A physical stamp in the passport, or document granted by a US Embassy or Consulate outside the US, that permits the recipient to approach the US border and request permission to enter the US in a particular immigrant or nonimmigrant status.

visa process: A nonimmigrant or immigrant application submitted to the US Embassy or Consulate to obtain an immigrant or nonimmigrant visa.

Fargo Students' Traveling Exhibit

Twenty of these students' stories are featured in a traveling exhibit, available to schools, universities, libraries, and other venues where communities gather. The exhibit features twenty banners, each with a portrait, a 200-word biography, and a quote from each immigrant. A QR code is displayed next to each portrait and can be scanned with a mobile device to watch the digital stories. The following programming can be provided with the exhibit: panel discussions, presentations, and community-building events.

Green Card Voices currently has five exhibits based on different communities across the Midwest. To rent an exhibit, please contact us at 612.889.7635 or info@greencardvoices.com.

Green Card Youth Voices: Book Readings

Meeting the student authors in person creates a dynamic space in which to engage with these topics firsthand. Book readings are a wonderful opportunity to hear the students share their stories and answer questions about their lived experiences.

To schedule a book reading in your area, please contact us at 612.889.7635 or info@greencardvoices.com.

About Green Card Voices

Founded in 2013, Green Card Voices (GCV) is a nonprofit organization that utilizes digital storytelling to share personal narratives of America's immigrants, establishing a better understanding between the immigrant and nonimmigrant population. Our dynamic, video-based platform is designed to empower a variety of educational institutions, community groups, and individuals to acquire a first-person perspective about immigrants' lives, increasing the appreciation of the immigrant experience in America.

Green Card Voices was born from the idea that the broad narrative of current immigrants should be communicated in a way that is true to each immigrant's story. We seek to be a new lens for those in the immigration dialogue and build a bridge between immigrants and nonimmigrants—newcomers and the receiving community—from across the country. We do this by sharing the firsthand immigration stories of foreign-born Americans, by helping others to see the "wave of immigrants" as individuals, with interesting stories of family, hard work, and cultural diversity.

To date, the Green Card Voices team has recorded the life stories of almost three hundred immigrants coming from over 100 different countries. All immigrants that decide to share their story with GCV are asked six open-ended questions. In addition, they are asked to share personal photos of their life in their country of birth and in the US. The video narratives are edited down to five-minute videos filled with personal photographs, an intro, an outro, captions, and background music. These video stories are available on www.greencardvoices.org, and YouTube (free of charge and advertising).

Green Card Youth Voices: Immigration Stories from a Fargo High School is the second in a series of many books that GCV hopes to publish in other cities as well; future series that we are working on include: *Green Card Entrepreneur Voices* and *Green Card Artist Voices*.

Contact information:
Green Card Voices
2822 Lyndale Ave S
55408 Minneapolis, MN

www.greencardvoices.org
612.889.7635

Facebook: www.facebook.com/GreenCardVoices
Twitter: www.twitter.com/GreenCardVoices

Now available:

Green Card Youth Voices:
Immigration Stories from a Minneapolis High School

The first book in the Green Card Youth Voices series, *Green Card Youth Voices: Immigration Stories from a Minneapolis High School* is a unique book of personal essays written by students from Wellstone International High School. Coming from 13 different countries, these young people share stories of family, school, change, and dreams. The broad range of experiences and the honesty with which these young people tell their stories is captured here with inspiring clarity. Available as an ebook (ISBN: 978-0-9974960-1-7) and paperback (ISBN : 978-0-9974960-0-0).

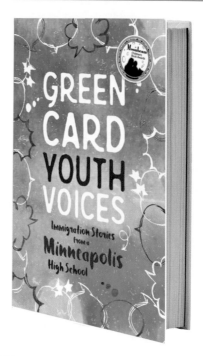

Recipient of the 2016 Moonbeam Children's Gold Medal for Multicultural Non-Fiction Chapter Book

Contents:
- Full color portraits
- 30 personal essays by students from around the world
- Links to digital video stories on the Green Card Voices website
- Foreword by Kao Kalia Yang, award-winning author of *The Latehomecomer* and *The Song Poet*
- Excerpt from *Act4Change: A Green Card Voices Study Guide*
- Glossary

To purchase online and view a list of retailers, visit greencardvoices.org/books.

Also available on Amazon.

146

Green Card Youth Voices:
Immigration Stories from a St. Paul High School

Based on the successful model used in Minneapolis, MN and Fargo, ND, *Green Card Youth Voices: Immigration Stories from a St. Paul High School* features 30 student authors from LEAP High School and is a vehicle to generate awareness about the immigrant experience. The book includes links to the students' video narrative, a study guide, and glossary to help teachers use the book as an educational resource when teaching about immigration. Available as an ebook (ISBN: 978-0-9974960-5-5) and paperback (ISBN : 978-0-9974960-3-1).

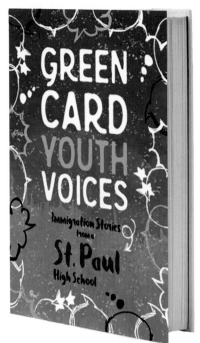

Contents:

- Full color portraits
- 30 personal essays by students from around the world
- Links to digital video stories on the Green Card Voices website
- Excerpt from *Act4Change: A Green Card Voices Study Guide*
- Glossary

To purchase online and view a list of retailers, visit greencardvoices.org/books.

Also available on Amazon.

Also Available:

Voices of Immigrant Storytellers:
A Teaching Guide for Middle and High Schools

This 10-lesson curriculum based on the Common Core standards was written and designed by immigrants. The teaching guide progressively unfolds the humanity, diversity, and contributions of new American citizens and siutates students' own stories alongside these narratives using eleven Green Card Voices' video narratives. This teaching guide is adaptable for grades 6-12. Available as an ebook (ISBN: 978-0-692-51151-0) and paperback (ISBN : 978-0-692-57281-8).

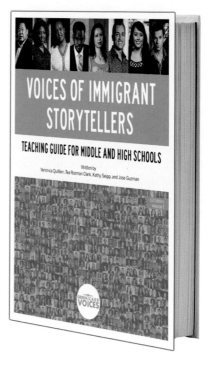

Includes:
- 72 illustrated pages
- 11 Green Card Voices Stories
- 7 ready-to-use worksheets
- 8 classroom activities
- 2 field trip suggestions
- 20 online resources

Available at
greencardvoices.org/books
teacherspayteachers.com
amazon.com

For more information, visit our website at www.greencardvoices.org
or contact us at info@greencardvoices.com

Order Form

To order more copies of *Green Card Youth Voices: Immigration Stories from a Fargo High School, Voices of Immigrant Storytellers: Teaching Guide for Middle and High Schools,* and/or one of our other books, visit www.greencardvoices.org/books or fill out the order form below and deliver it to:

Green Card Voices
2822 Lyndale Ave. S.
Minneapolis, MN 55408

Title	Quantity	Price	Total
Green Card Youth Voices: Immigration Stories from a ST. PAUL High School		x $20.00	
Green Card Youth Voices: Immigration Stories from a FARGO High School		x $20.00	
Green Card Youth Voices: Immigration Stories from a MINNEAPOLIS High School		x $20.00	
Voices of Immigrant Storytellers: Teaching Guide for Middle and High Schools		x $19.99	
* Please include $4.00 shipping ***per book.***		Shipping*	
		TOTAL	

Name: _____

Address: _____

City: _____ State: _____ Zip: _____

Phone: _____

Email: _____

☐ Check enclosed   ☐ Cash enclosed   ☐ Credit Card Order
Checks made to
Green Card Voices

Card Number: _____ Card Security Code: _____

Expiration Date: _____/_____ Name on Card: _____

GREEN CARD
VOICES

2822 Lyndale Ave S. Minneapolis, MN
ww.greencardvoices.org
612.889.7635